D0786859

A THEORY

OF

FAMILY SYSTEMS

# A THEORY
# OF
# FAMILY SYSTEMS

*Norman J. Ackerman, M.D.*

GARDNER PRESS, INC.
*New York & London*

Gardner Press, Inc.
19 Union Square West
New York 10003

All foreign orders except Canada and South America to:
Afterhurst Limited
Chancery House
319 City Road
London N1, United Kingdom

Library of Congress Cataloging in Publication Data
Ackerman, Norman J.
    A theory of family systems.
    Bibliography: p.
    Includes index.
    1. Family therapy.    2. Social systems — Therapeutic
use.    I. Title.
RC488.5.A26      1984      616.89'156      83-5668
ISBN 0-89876-032-1

ILLUSTRATIONS BY ALDO PELLINI
DESIGN BY RAYMOND SOLOMON
PRINTED IN THE UNITED STATES OF AMERICA

*To my wife and children,*
  *To my parents,*
    *To my grandparents and aunts,*
*To our clan and your clan and the families*
  *of our children's children.*

# ACKNOWLEDGMENTS

Nathan Ward Ackerman, Nat as he liked to be called, gave me the space, literally and figuratively, to be a family therapist. I started practice with him, sharing families and groups, in 1961. I also taught at the Family Mental Health Clinic which he established at the Jewish Family Service in New York, so that, when I went to the Family Studies Section of the Bronx Psychiatric Center (Albert Einstein College of Medicine) in 1969, my presence and style were well-formed.

I was not satisfied with my theoretical base, however, and, when Tom Fogarty and I recognized a basic affinity for one another, I enthusiastically engaged in a two-year weekly dialogue with him, often in the presence of students and various colleagues of the Section. He taught me about triangles, and I created the idea of the threesome. We both wrestled with the inadequacies of fusion. I continued with my seminars and students to refine and eventually overhaul fusion, added insulation, and reworked triangulation. The latter work was done largely with two of my then-fellows, Bill McFarlane and Ken Terkelsen, who spent many hours with me producing a training videotape on triangulation.[1] They also read early drafts of chapters two, three, and four and made many suggestions. Jim

[1]Down on Jack Night, Family Video Productions, 1975.

Jennings, originally a student and then a partner also read many of the chapters and critiqued them with diligence and discernment. Dick Fulmer, a student and then assistant teacher in my How to Teach Seminar, not only read the main chapters but also took the trouble to write a practical summary of the concepts and notation. All of these people have supported me with dedication and love as do my associates at the Creedmoor Family Institute, Wendy Blair, Jackie Velazquez, and Dan Wiener, with whom these ideas were further refined. I owe much to my hundreds of students over the years, who are always willing to challenge, investigate, and question. And, of course, this book itself acknowledges the thousands of families that have given me the privilege of membership.

I thank Genevieve Vaughn for efforts far above and beyond the norm for a copyeditor and for improving much of the phrasing and sentence structure. Raymond and Sidney Solomon, the designers and producers, functioned as a fine team, with Ray doing the design work and Sidney willing to listen and advise at any time. Aldo Pellini did a yeoman's job of rendering the many figures accurately and artistically. Gardner Spungin, my publisher, was patient at the right times, pressing at the right times and always a quiet, positive force.

As many an author has discovered, there is no way a project of this kind gets done without a support group, usually a family. The process itself is a testimony to the power of family. In my own instance, my family, immediate and extended, lived with and kept the idea of a book alive for fourteen years. This, my father and mother and aunt and wife and children did despite the fact that, until very recently, I was practically insupportable. The gift of being able to be supported which has emerged during the process I value far greater than the product.

I thank my son, Ken, especially, for his ever-present good cheer.

Lastly, I thank Dorothy, my wife, for her unfailing courage, inspiration, and love.

# PREFACE

This is an offering of a theory and a model (map is the current word in vogue) of families and family therapy. Although it owes much to many thinkers and clinicians, I own it all, for better or worse. It is a more complete theory than most that I know (some of which are collections of concepts without much inter-relationship), and therefore more pleasing or aesthetic, but I must confess that my intended result in publishing is that it will be pragmatic.

Whether it be utilitarian or beautiful seems a nonsense question. "For art comes to you proposing frankly to give nothing but the highest quality to your moments as they pass, and simply for those moments' sake."[1] And what could be more useful than that, to enhance life or living itself? And who can deny that any improvement in function must lend itself to increase the possibility of pleasure, of joy, of the appreciation of life? Art is useful, and what works is beautiful.

Although much of the material was written for the first time in 1970 for my own benefit and I have been long since interested in other matters entirely, my students and colleagues have insisted that the treatment is current and cogent and that

[1]Walter Pater, *The Renaissance, Studies in Art and Poetry* (London: Macmillan and Co., 1910), 239.

it is a theory that "one can put in one's pocket when one sits with a family and use it at will." I do not doubt this. My question is whether any theory can be assimilated out of a book in such a way that it enhances therapeutic skills without going through the training program which it represents. We shall see.

I recommend that in reading this theory, you be willing to come to it afresh rather than try to categorize it in terms of theories which are already familiar; otherwise, you will miss that which is different and valuable.

I also recommend that you not try to learn the doing of family therapy from a book such as this. Rather, get a good teacher, immerse yourself in families for a few years and then go back and integrate a theory that suits you.

The first chapter establishes a context for the rest of the book. The second, third, and fourth are the basic theory. The fifth and sixth are major theoretical branches of the basic theory. Chapter seven was reprinted to demonstrate the clinical applications of the theory. Chapters eight and nine address the distinctions between style and technique and, more importantly, demonstrate that this theory is inclusive and useful regardless of style or technique of the therapist. (I do suggest that we therapists quit calling every new technique a new theory.) Finally, Chapter ten recapitulates the theory and some clinical applications in outline form.

I use the word canon to convey the immutability of the rules of family process and there is no difficulty for me in also stating that the theory is wholly made up. The law of gravity *and* the law of relativity are immutable and both are made up and different, one from the other. Moreover, just as the dependability and unforgivingness of gravity allows for a full expression of Self as in dancing, so the canon of family systems allows for the richness and variety of patterns of living.

I have worked and reworked Murray Bowen's original triangulation process until it now is significantly different and perhaps should have a new name. I honor Murray in the process of modifying his ideas. Likewise, fusion I use only in an interactional and descriptive sense.

Insulation as an always and only complement to fusion is entirely my own as is my schema for intergenerational transmission. The latter comes out of my work with therapists' own families and much study of the work system as consultant and trainer. How we recreate our families of origin in the workplace is a most valuable aspect of the theory and deserves another book.

The idea of the threesome as the basic unit of health and the criteria of health are entirely mine and are the core of the theory.

Finally, dear reader, let me thank you for tarrying with me awhile. Warm yourself by the fire, taste as much as you want, digest what you like, leave what you don't. Above all, take everything in the spirit of questioning. If this book solves problems I will be disappointed. If it opens up new questions, it will serve its purpose.

*Norman J. Ackerman, M.D.*
*Kings Point, New York*

# CONTENTS

CHAPTER **I**
# THE IDEA OF THE FAMILY

**t**he idea of the family, particularly from the point of view of family therapy, was spawned in the fifties, developed in the sixties and had become a bandwagon in the seventies. In the eighties it will be laid to rest. That is to say, like all human enterprises, having broken through the initial resistance and having survived the deification of its disciples, it now finds its rightful usage, neither panacea nor hoax. At the same time, as an accepted body of knowledge, the family approach now becomes codified and reified, and the wildly exciting period of continual new growth is over. Henceforth, each truly creative step will require an effortful and sometimes painful breakthrough. This process is neither good nor bad; it is simply inevitable.

I mourn the days of "healthy, unstructured state of chaos" (1), when every observation was an automatic breakthrough, and am at heart an antitheorist who eschews the possible deadening effect of being ultraproficient technically or too

1

facile conceptually. "Doing something about it" is often far removed from the experience we want to do something about, and "thinking about something" is often a very poor substitute for knowing. Relying on theory is a surefire way of avoiding the experience of actually being with a family and seeing anew what is happening. Truly being with a family is a necessary condition for powerful, growth-enhancing therapy.

Nonetheless, we all do theorize willy-nilly, and the exercise of trying or pretending not to theorize—the analogue of telling oneself, "I am not thinking of an elephant"—is as debilitating as becoming embedded in one's concepts. The trick, then, is to allow our minds to theorize freely, recognize the results as wholly made-up constructs, be neither enamored of them nor wed to them, use them when useful, and be totally willing to discard them when they get in the way or when something better comes along. The paradox is that if one can become totally free to theorize, one can become free of theory. I therefore offer these contributions to the general idea of the family with the recommendation that the reader bear in mind that they are wholly made up by me or someone else, and that they need not be cherished or revered. Holding this body of principles in this manner will enhance the burgeoning of family therapy. Holding it as truth from on high will hasten the petrification of family therapy.

## The Family as Part of a Hierarchy

During the next decade, we shall also come to see that family therapy is but a part of the larger idea of the family whose time has come. This idea or context is a manifestation of the evolution of the human Self as mankind moves from the idea of the individual through the idea of relationship to the idea of family or group and confronts the idea of clan or community. Just as psychoanalysis grew out of the Age of Enlightenment, with its emphasis on the individual, so family therapy has grown out of the present period's phenomenal technological explosion, with its attendant concerns for nurturing, loss of values, and tradition. Sandwiched in between the two major preoccupations of individual and family was, and still is, a natural focusing on dyadic relationships (as in Buber's I and Thou and Sullivan's psychology of the interpersonal).

The speed of this evolution has been too swift to fully apprehend its impact on our world. Even as we begin to appreciate ourselves and others on the level of group or family, we see that if we are to make a contribution to families in general, we must master the context of families. Thus we begin to prepare ourselves for the quantum leap of experiencing ourselves and others on the level of clan, community, or organization. Now we need to know, in addition to the rules of small groups, the rules of the relationships among groups. And the well-being of the human species on a global level can only be served by organizations of organizations (a level beyond community that I call the level of *institution*). If we are to have a livable world (at least for humans), we will need to encompass all of these levels in the not too distant future.

## Family Includes Individual

From this point of view, the rules of family are but a small piece of the whole, a steppingstone to further expansion. We need not be awed by the complexity of family, nor view mastery of family as a final solution to human ills. In addition, one must be clear that the growth of awareness is spherical rather than linear. When we move on to family, we do not leave individual psychology behind; rather, the idea of family *includes* the idea of the individual.

This last point cannot be stressed too much. Even as we look beyond family, we must realize that the world of therapy moves with the rest of the world, which is still in transit from the approach of linear causality to a more holistic point of view. The natural resistance to this passage is manifested not only by adherence to old notions and disparagement of new ones, but also by refusal to acknowlede or use time-tested constructs that still work. On the one hand, some psychoanalysts still regard family therapy as superficial, and some do not even want to know directly about the family of someone they are treating, for fear of "contaminating the analysis." On the other hand, some "systems thinkers" still avoid engaging individuals in therapy, for fear of taking sides or becoming embroiled in content.

That these two positions are two sides of the same coin is an acknowledgment of the power of the idea of the individual and of the degree to which we are still encumbered by mechanistic or linear cause-and-effect thinking. This is true of all of us. The mind does not think in wholes, at least not yet. My children have some sense that they and the mosquito partake of the same world. I have no such ecological sense. To me, one zaps the mosquito with DDT and that is that. I don't use DDT because I've been told it's "bad," but I do not grasp deep down that the loss of any bug is a loss to the environment, let alone to me.

All our early attempts to grasp the essence of family process led to linear concepts. Complementarity, interlocking pathology, and positive feedback are all examples of one-to-one thinking. "Circular causality" is no great breakthrough. One of the earliest notions encompassing three individuals is that of scapegoating in the service of a power struggle. This still contains within it a false cause, in that it leads automatically to viewing the process as a perpetration of two against one. Even the more abstract concept of triangulation discussed in Chapter V, which is not intrinsically linear, is used by many Bowenians in a linear fashion. One hears the phrase "being triangulated" and detects an attitude that this is bad and that one must bend all efforts to getting oneself "detriangulated." This last is a good example of how, even when we are thinking "systems" (that is, beyond linear cause and effect), our attitude may nevertheless be one of seeking cause, and our experience, one of blaming or feeling victimized.

## The Difficulty of Grasping the Whole

All this is not bad. It simply is, in my view, where most of us are with regard to family. We grasp the essence of family and lose it and grasp it and lose it again and again. Our words pale alongside our vision and, having difficulty articulating what we see, we can neither hold it nor communicate it. The trouble is that we then take refuge in "explaining" things with our mechanistic notions or, for fear of losing our overall view, we pretend that people and their inner systems do not exist.

The first route leads to the use of gimmicky techniques or the aping of a master therapist, rather than to the direct experience of oneself in relation to a family and, ultimately, to actually knowing what works for you and them. In order to reach certainty, one needs to be willing to go through a period of not knowing and confusion. The second route, the ignoring of inner systems, can lead to refusal to engage people and to lack of compassion, and it may have disastrous results. Minuchin cites such a case with the comment that "it is undesirable, uneconomical and sometimes ethically or humanly incorrect to ignore the other subsystems entirely" (2). In this case, the "other subsystem," a disabled fourteen-year-old boy, who was very much attached to his mother, was ignored by the therapist, who convinced the parents to go out by themselves and to continue going out despite a strong reaction by the boy. The first time they went out, the boy slashed his clothes with a razor. The second time, the boy broke a window, cutting his wrist, and walked the streets naked. The strategy fit the theory, not the family. This therapist, like many others, was not relating to the family directly, possibly for fear of being "sucked into the system," an often-heard rationalization. An acceptable direction for both therapist and family will be found if we are willing to experience ourselves as helpless to move a family in a direction it does not wish to go.

Many of our time-honored concepts and techniques have worked well and can continue to work — acceptance of Einsteinian theory does not mean we can no longer use Newtonian mechanics. In the above example, had the therapist simply seen the boy alone, he or she might have discovered the boy's fragility directly and even given the boy enough attention or offered some control, so that the boy need not have acted out. Instead, the therapist slavishly held to a strategy born purely out of family theory. The words "individual therapist" are spoken somewhat disparagingly in some family therapy training centers, but an individually oriented therapist would not have made this particular mistake. The idea of the family includes the idea of the individual, and young family therapists need not be ashamed to pay attention to intrapsychic processes. Moreover, a good family theory needs to be consistent with what we know about individuals.

## We Are Individualists First

If we can accept ourselves as individualists under the skin, it might make the passage easier. How could it be otherwise? The struggle to transcend the view of man as a chip on the waves of Natural Law took centuries, and even after the impetus of the Industrial Revolution there were still many misgivings about individual rights. Just prior to the Industrial Age, enlightened men like Madison needed to frame the Constitution to "prevent the majority from ever dominating the minority of the opulent" (3). Soon after the age began, the question of using children as beasts of burden in the collieries of England was seriously debated (4). Now that we are finally willing to recognize the responsiblity and rights of individuals and enjoy our Horatio Algers and Supermen, we are called on to recognize a larger collective. Of course we are going to be competitive. Of course we are going to find an underdog. Of course we are going to bridle at anything that smacks of authoritarian encroachment of freedom. Of course we are going to sympathize with the prevalent attitude of "I've gotta be me!" Or we will have to suppress our thoughts and feelings and take an opposing position, one that ignores the individual. If we can come from the point of view of family as context, then we can *have* our individualistic and anti-individualistic prejudices, rather than be run by them. We can be aware of our thoughts and feelings and not have to act upon them. Again, the idea of the family can contain all of this.[1]

[1]See von Bertalanffy's parallel discussion of the analytic mind versus the synthetic mind in his "Essay on the Relativity of Categories" (5).

## Family as Context

What is the idea of the family? First of all, it is a context. It belongs to that class of abstractions that Buckminster Fuller calls *generating principles*. These are extremely deep-seated, often unconscious, fundamental attitudes out of which we form our perceptions and, hence, they govern our experience of ourselves and the world. The abstracton of family (or small group) is *me, not me, and not not me.*[2] Out of this abstraction comes the awareness of *me, not me, and not not me* as a unit of interaction. This becomes the experience of self as *you-and-me-and-other* in relation to *them*. Finally, there comes the realization that our fates are inextricably intertwined with at least two significant others, that we do not go it alone, and that it really is "all for one and one for all."

*Human Growth — Taking on Levels of Increasing Responsibility*

In order to move from the mystification of the idea of Natural Law to the enlightenment of the idea of the individual, humanity had to become conscious of thoughts, emotions, and body sensations, as distinguished from observations. The philosophers of the Age of Enlightenment spent a great deal of time considering perception — getting clear, for example, that "beauty is in the eye of the beholder." In human growth, as in biology, ontogeny recapitulates phylogeny: Each person in the course of his or her development must become more aware of the workings of mind and body and must "own" them if he or she is to have the rights and responsibilities of an individual. The alternative is to remain a victim, blaming circumstances for our reactions and being helpless in the face of them. (Actually, blaming circumstances can occur only after awareness of one's undesired reactions is present, and this blame therefore represents the first step toward assuming responsibility

[2]I am indebted to Werner Erhard and Randy MacNamara of Werner Erhard Associates for the articulation and communication of this abstraction.

for self as an individual.) As one becomes more clear about one's thoughts, emotions, and body sensations, one confronts being responsible for them, and if one is willing to relinquish blame, one begins to master oneself as an individual.

Even as this process commences, one's attention turns toward relationships. Now, the inner processes are no longer obscured; but barriers come up between individuals, so that communications are blocked. It is difficult to see the other's point of view and even more difficult to "get through." Barriers are idiosyncratic reactions to the fear of taking on a new area of responsibility and are therefore indicators of new growth.

At this point, one may be willing to be fully responsible for self as individual, but unwilling to be responsible for self as relationship. The fundamental attitude is "it's you or me." Even when it is couched in benign, reasonable terms, such as "I am perfectly happy to have you do your thing so long as I am free to do mine" (to paraphrase Fritz Perls), there is implicit in this attitude an unwillingness to take responsibility for the relationship as such or to make a commitment. In practice, the hedge of "taking *my* 50 percent" quickly degenerates into an agreement contingent upon the other's taking *his* 50 percent. The result is to avoid responsibility and place oneself at the effect of the other, another variation of the blame game. (Why should I hold up my end if you don't hold up yours?) It's not bad to be unwilling to take responsibility. It simply doesn't work. The relationship may survive and tasks may be accomplished, but the participants will gain neither satisfaction nor increased vitality. On the other hand, one can walk away from relationships, and the job will not get done.

As for parents and siblings, one is born committed to them, and to walk away from them is to bog oneself down in the past, forever incapacitating oneself in order to prove them wrong. The only way out of this morass is to be willing to make the relationship work for the other, to take it on 100 percent, to see one's interests as joined to the other's, to hold the relationship in the context of you *and* me. If one can come from this point of view, one ceases to make the other wrong, communications flow naturally, and all the "issues" that previously seemed insurmountable now dissolve. There is no longer a blurring of boundaries, a confusion as to who is who. Each person is equally clear about his or her own experience and about the other person's experience and knows that the two cannot be the same. Each now has the opportunity to provide new data to the other, and the relationship becomes creative as well as mutual and cooperative.

This idyllic condition is no sooner realizable than one confronts the need to include another in the relationship. The world does not let one shut it out. Now the relationship appears threatened, and the barriers come up again as one views the situation as us or other — as one confronts unwillingness to be responsible for self as group or as family and resorts to suppressing the other.

The rules of this process and the evolvement of a well-functioning threesome constitute the content of this book. If one tries to keep a relationship the way it is, it goes to pot. A relationship that is about making the relationship work demands that there be problems in the relationship. On the other hand, the responsibility of making a group or family work is awesome, and no one takes it on easily. Many a mature, well-put-together person has failed to make this passage. One difficulty is that whenever one confronts a new area of responsibility, one's idiosyncratic barriers get reactivated. These take the form of familiar old symptoms that lend themselves to the assumption that one is going backwards if one doesn't know one is going forward. The mind is simplistic. What worked before should work again. If becoming more aware of thoughts and feelings worked before, do it again. If being in therapy worked before, do it again.

Many people who remain perennial patients are actually, I believe, people who have been on the threshold of new growth and have not recognized it. Many of my patients have returned to me years after having completed therapy successfully, prepared to go another round because they are experiencing old familiar symptoms and figure they are "back to square one." Investigation reveals that their original problems have remained cleared up, and that they are now operating on a much higher level. Pointing this out to the patient not only may save the person from going down a blind alley, but it also facilitates new growth. One woman had come into therapy because her alcoholic husband would not. Her therapy was very successful when she terminated. Not only had she handled her own reactions on many fronts, but her relationship with her husband was also excellent, and he had stopped drinking. She had also made dramatic changes in her relationship to her family of grown children who, in turn, had improved their functioning. When she returned because of anxiety, fatigue, and insomnia, she was fully ready for a "refresher course." I found, however, that her relationships and family were holding up very well, and that her main preoccupation was now with the difficulties involved in negotiating as an official of her church with officials of another church regarding an international refugee problem. She was quite frustrated and contemplated giving up the whole project in disgust. She was totally identified with her own organization and unwilling to take on responsibility on the next higher level of institution. When she got in touch with her attitude of "who needs *them!*" the whole episode dissolved, including her symptoms, and she successfully managed the situation in question for the benefit of both organizations. My only role was to encourage her to accept her frustration and anger for two sessions.

And so, when one does take on responsibility for self as family or group, when one does acknowledge the *not not me's* as well as the *not me*, one begins to master being supported by a group — and immediately notices that one's group relates to other groups. The cycle of growth begins anew (see Table 1.1). The idea of family is now the content for the context called the idea of clan or community.

## The Larger Picture

Family is viewed, then, as part of an open, hierarchical system, what Koestler terms a *holon* (6). It is a defined entity in its own right with its own rules. It is a whole with respect to its individuals and a part with respect to its clan. The same considerations apply to individuals and clans. A basic as-

**Table 1.1.**

**Anatomy of Hierarchical Levels of People Systems**

(Applies to all interpenetrating systems; for example, kinship, work, church, government)

| Level | Interface (Area of Barriers)[a] | Experience of Barrier | Condition of Survival[b] | Maintenance Process[c] | Unconscious Attitude | Responsibility Achieved by |
|---|---|---|---|---|---|---|
| Individual | me-and-mindbody | confusion, out-of-touchness | unconsciousness | repression | I am my mind | observation of mind |
| Relationship | you-and-me | stuckness (burden or humiliation) | barricading (entanglement) | blame | I and my mindbody are sufficient | making other right (no fault) |
| Family (or group, department) | us-and-other | inhibition (subversion) | fusion-insulation | suppression (disqualification, undermining, double-binding, triangulation) | relationship is *it* | acknowledgment of all |
| Clan (or community, organization) | us-and-them | estrangement (murderous competition) | cliquiness (gang formation) | ostracism or engulfment with disciple formation | family is private, privileged and no one else is trustworthy | participation and invitation |
| Tribe (or institution; large corporation, military, or judiciary) | our operation and theirs | alienation (ridicule, disparagement) | jargonism | absorption with subordination | the clan takes care of its own —only | cooperation mutual support |
| Nation (or government, religion, or race) | our mission and theirs | superior zeal (benign disdain) | confidentiality, secrecy | competitive production and duplication | we know best | dissemination and exploration |
| Society (humanity) | our planet and theirs | patriotism and superstition | isolationism | massive effort to outperform | we deserve more or better | sharing, redistributing resources |

[a]Barriers arise as one approaches the experience of self at the next level (of growth).

[b]Refers to survival of *prior* level. For example, one does give up the sanctity of the individual self when one takes on responsibility as relationship, and the fear is that individuality will be lost. At the next level, fusion is an attempt to preserve the relationship, out of fear that it may be destroyed by a third party.

[c]Mostly homeostatic mechanisms to keep conditions as they are.

sumption about family process, therefore, is that a change in family process produces a change in the individual and clan, just as surely as a change in the individual or clan will effect a change in the family. Years ago, Murray Bowen said that he elected "to leave integration of individual and family concepts for some future generation" in order to avoid "non-productive cyclical debates" (7). This is actually not possible. Family and individual are integrated in life, and if our observations of them are correct, the observations, too, will be integrated.

Another basic assumption is that the state of any individual in a family at any given time is a function of the sum of the states of all other individuals at that time. This statement defines the family. Clinically, it means that effecting a change in any one relationship within a family effects a change in all other relationships within the family. Putting the two basic assumptions together, it is evident that intervention at any level can have impact for all. Many years ago, Ruth Easser, in a large survey of people who had completed psychoanalysis, found that a major constant correlate of successful analysands was a marked change in their perceptions of their family of origin (8). In these instances, the major form of intervention was transference interpretation that had an indirect, unintentional effect on family interaction. (This effect, incidentally, was not used as a criterion of success either by analysand or analyst.) At the other end of the spectrum, time and time again I have observed profound psychodynamic changes that have occurred in the wake of simple shifts in family interaction. A mother who is very tied to and burdened by her child will ultimately exhibit, for example, remarkable shifts in her intrapsychic processes if her husband begins to "relieve" her by taking on more of the parenting.

The human spirit is forever concocting dualisms. Like "nature or nurture?" the question "individual or family?" is a false one. In practice, all individual therapists "treat" the family, like it or not; and all family therapists use the judgments and insights of individual psychology as they engage the people in a family, whether they are aware of it or not. As therapists, we would do well to include as much in our armamentarium as we can muster and to encompass as wide a view as we can hold. It is time for us to get rid of the us-or-them attitude in the mental health field. In this spirit, I wish to look more closely at family functioning. "Individual *versus* family" is a needless limitation. The idea of the family has room for both.

# References

1. Bowen, Murray, "The Use of Family Theory in Clinical Practice," *Comprehensive Psychiatry, 7* (1966), 347.

2. Minuchin, Salvador, *Families and Family Therapy* (Cambridge, Mass.: Harvard University Press, 1974), 106.

3. Jacobson, J. Mark, *The Development of American Political Thought: A Documentary History* (The Century Co., 1932), 164-79, quoted in Billington, Ray Allen, Loewenberg, Bert James, Brokunier, Hugh Samuel, *The Making of American Democracy* (New York: Rinehart & Co., 1950), 107.

4. Cooper, Anthony Ashley, 7th Earl of Shaftesbury, Speech in the House of Commons, June 7, 1842, reprinted in *Speeches of the Earl of Shaftesbury, K.G.* (London: Champan & Hall, 1868), 31-58, quoted in William Kessen, *The Child* (New York: John Wiley, 1965), 45-56.

5. Bertalanffy, Ludwig von, "An Essay on the Relativity of Categories," *Philosophy of Science, 22* (1955), 243-63.

6. Koestler, Arthur, *The Ghost in the Machine* (New York: Macmillan, 1967), 450-58.

7. Bowen, "Family Theory," 355.

8. Easser, Ruth, Personal communication, survey of patients of Columbia Psychoanalytic Clinic for Training and Research, 1962.

**II**

# THE FAMILY AND GENERAL SYSTEM THEORY

**a** number of authors, among them, Menninger et al. (1), von Bertalanffy (2), Grinker (3), and Gray et al. (4), have introduced correlations of general system theory and psychology. Family therapists have been especially interested, because traditional dynamics do not fully explain the behavior of tightly organized groups. The word *system* has been bandied about, and there is much agreement that the family is a system, but until recently little effort has been made to inquire either whether or in what way the family has the formal attributes of a system. Attempting to make psychoanalytic language fit general system theory (5) is precisely *not* using general system theory. Such attempts confirm what is already known rather than adding anything new. This is important because if the principles of regulation found in other natural organizations can be applied to families, more useful hypotheses can be made. Moreover, such usage should point the way to look for new data that would be missed with older models. If families are truly natural systems, we should be able to discern ways to make accurate predictions of human behavioral patterns.

It is appropriate, then, to compare what we know about families with general system theory and see if there is a fit. Let us look at systems and families and see whether function in one corresponds to function in the other. We want to know if the processes first found in biological organisms and described by von Bertalanffy in general terms are to be observed in families.

## System and Family Defined

According to von Bertalanffy, a system is "entities standing in interaction" (6). This means that any group of entities constitutes a system if change in behavior of any entity is a function of the sum of the behavior of all other entities. Certainly, families exhibit what have been called constitutive characteristics, rather than summative characteristics. This means that the group varies with its components' relationships rather than with numbers. When a child is born to a couple, it is a brand-new group, not the same group with an addition. When a parent is lost (or a child), the same is true. A family is distinguished by its parts together with their relationships, and it behaves as a whole, not as an aggregate.

I would define a family as a household in which the behavior of any one person is at all times a function of behavior of all other members. This means that change in the behavior of any one person affects all the other people in a meaningful way. *Meaningful* can be understood here as resulting in observable change in behavior. This is opposed to a mob, for instance, which is an aggregate of entities rather than a system; in a mob, the loss or addition of a member is simply that, and it results in no observable change in the nature of the mob but only a change in its strength. I use the original familia of household as a convenient distinction from other small groups and networks (which would include extended family), because I am not yet sure how best to separate those systems of people whose members have constant meaningful effects on one another from those systems whose members have either occasional effects or effects only in the actual presence of one another. Yet *household* is not an ideal word, because a family system may include, for example, a grandmother living in another apartment or house near the nuclear family, or a youngster living away at school.

In these instances, as Campbell (7) has pointed out, we are very skilled at discerning whether or not such members are part of the basic family system. What we observe is that there is considerable process[1] going on between such members and members of the household, and/or that the relationship of at least two members of a household varies when there is a variation in the relationship of either member with the member outside the household. Ashby, in his discussion of conditionality (8), observes that these phenomena may represent two aspects of systems relatedness: "As soon as the relation between two entities A and B becomes conditional on C's value or state, then a necessary component of organization is present." Later, he adds: "This way of looking at 'conditionality' makes us realize that it is related to that of 'communication'; and it is, of course, quite plausible that we should define parts as being 'organized' when 'communication' (in some generalized sense) occurs between them."

I assume that the "generalized sense" of communication would correspond with the word process as I use it here. I would further suggest that my "considerable process" would be that amount of process required to produce conditionality as a constant feature of the relationships as opposed to an

[1]By *process* I mean either communication in the formal sense (transmission of bits) or matter-energy exchange as carefully described by Miller (9). These always occur together but, clinically, one predominates. Usually, communication would be most important in maintaining the relatedness of an outside household member, but not necessarily. An emigrant father leaving his family behind, for example, might maintain his position in the family mainly by sending back money, goods, or food.

occasional feature and that this, in turn, would define von Bertalanffy's phrase "standing in interaction." For example, a non-family-member relationship could occasionally affect a family relationship — as in the instance of the loss of an intimate friend (which could increase the family member's interaction with the family) — but any change in the relationship of spouses would invariably affect the parent-child relationships.

## General System Processes Manifested by Families

Let us now proceed to examine each of the fundamental processes of a system in relation to family. As we do, bear in mind that each of these processes represents gradual transitions of an organism to an end point or final steady state. They are the abstractions of the phenomena of growth and aging.

*Progressive segregation* is a term given to that process whereby an organization is built up out of a uniform whole by differentiation of parts increasingly independent of one another. The prototype of this process is the formation of an embryo from a single cell by the splitting of cells and the gradual specialization of cells. So long as there remains some interdependence of parts, there remains regulability of one part by another, but eventually each part becomes more fixed in its actions or less regulable by the actions of the other parts. This extreme of progressive segregation is called *progressive mechanization* and is manifested, for example, in aging and fragmentation.

Families organize similarly. Honeymooners are a uniform whole in many ways. Although role formation and complementary functioning actually begins when a couple meet (some aspects being culturally predetermined), it is generally after a couple set up housekeeping that more specific and independent functions come into being. The creation of children furthers the differentiation of the parents; and, just as in other systems, aging occurs by fragmentation, as youngsters become more autonomous and split off to form new families. As these individuals become more specialized, they become less regulable. They also become more interactive with other systems that border on the family (for example, peer groups, work groups, political groups). When the behavior of one member of the family becomes fixed with respect to the family, as in the case of a particularly estranged adolescent or a senile oldster, the family can no longer regulate itself and reestablish its balance (steady state). Clinically, this is manifested in relationship problems of other members of the family, symptom formation, and psychosomatic eruptions. In general, crisis prevails until the too-differentiated member is finally segregated (lost or expulsed) and the family can reorganize itself. Sometimes, however, the family breaks up over what might be considered a trivial event. Not infrequently, marital disruption occurs following a youngster's going off to school, corresponding to the end point of progressive segregation or mechanization.

*Centralization*, like segregation, is a time-dependent process. Here, leading parts form in such a way that small changes in the leading or dominant part produce large changes in other parts. *Triggers* is another name for dominant parts, and triggers follow the principle of instigative causality; that is, small energy changes can produce large energy results. The end point of progressive centralization is individualization. The organism becomes unified and indivisible; that is to say, the subordinate parts cease to have any autonomy and therefore can no longer be distinguished functionally from the dominant part. Families tend to do this when under pressure to respond with all strength available to a current need. In a financial crisis, for example, one member assumes dominance in the direction of all family activity toward producing and conserving money. Mortal illness of one member can result in the same sort of effort. Centralization is seen regularly when, at the birth of a child, all functions tend to be subordinated to nurturing. In this instance, other functions are kept going, though they are no longer in the foreground. When all but one of the primary family functions (10) are virtually excluded, centralization may be said to have become pathological. The classic example would be the mother-dominated family devoted to child-rearing alone, in which the child is in symbiotic position to the mother, and the father is relegated to an extreme, distant position, serving only to earn money to support the operation.

All social groups require leadership for identity and stability, and so it is with family. Self-styled "democratic" families are often chaotic bunches. Centralization, then, not only allows for more efficient functioning when major efforts are required, but it is also the cement that gives the family continuity. On the other hand, segregation — abundantly elaborated in one of its dimensions as role formation — (11), not only provides the specialization required for easy accomplishment of everyday tasks, but it also maintains differentiation of individual members against the coalescing tendency of centralization.

Progressive centralization and progressive segregation, in my view, are complementary processes. They occur simultaneously and are both aspects of growth in a family. The end points represent the demise of the family, for once a family has reached complete centralization or segregation, it is no longer a family. The major thrust of this book will be to demonstrate that these two constructs, together with the mechanism generally used to prevent them from reaching *extemis*, can be used to describe all family interaction. We shall call the end point of segregation in families *insulation* and the end point of centralization *fusion* (after Bowen, but not the same as his construct). The stabilizing process that prevents either segregation or centralization from reaching an end point is triangulation.

## Introduction to the Tripartite Theory of Fusion, Insulation and Triangulation

Characteristic of systems is that the functions are nonlinear. They are not simple causal chains, but organizations that must have at least three entities. So it is with families. The wholeness comes only with the formation of a relationship that is more than a meeting of two people. Taken into account is each person's history and extended family, as well as the world at large in relation to them as a pair. As Nathan W. Ackerman once said, "there is no such thing as two in a bed." There is always at least an audience. This point will be further elaborated in Chapter III, but for now I take it as axiomatic that two may be company but three's a family. If such be the case, fusion (end point of centralization) of two people in a family means that the third or others must either be insulated (end point of segregation) with respect to the fused pair or be a part of the fusion (See Figure 2.1). The first situation I term a psychotic family (the traditional diagnostician would label the insulated member psychotic). The second situation (all fused) corresponds to Bowen's "undifferentiated family ego mass" (12). The experience of a clinician being unable to gain entry into a family — Wynne's "rubber fence" phenomenon (13) — can be understood as the total unification of the family into a whole, leaving no individuals to address. I consider such a family externally psychotic or psychotic with respect to its community or clan.

Fusion and insulation are so-called mathematical ideals; that is to say, they are end points that are approached but never actually reached. (The paradox is that when these end points are reached, the systems involved are no longer the families

Figure 2.1

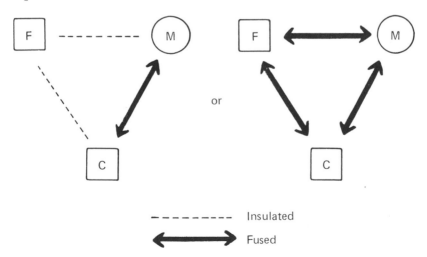

that started the process.) Fusion and insulation may be approximated periodically, however, with enough frequency to render the family dysfunctional. By far, however, what happens most often is that there develops a holding pattern called triangulation.

Triangulation will be elaborated on later (Chapter V), but it can be summarized as two persons relating through a third in such a way as to freeze their own relationship and prevent both insulation from one another and fusion with a third party (see Figure 2.2). The third person at this moment is treated as a thing (object of discussion, message transmitter, property), and there is little or no personal communication. (By personal communication, I mean the expression of belief or affect regarding the other of a pair.) The advantage of this arrangement is that it prevents the possibility that an end point will be reached, and the family remains intact — for while a pair are relating through a third person, they can neither get too close nor too distant. The problem is that triangulation barricades emotional give and take, prevents resolution of conflict, and stilts growth, especially in the so-called "triangulated" member. The greater the tendency for fusion or insulation in a threesome, the greater the need for triangulation, and the greater the dysfunction.

The price of holding a family together can be extremely high, but it is frequently paid as long as possible. The more inoperative one member is as a person, the easier it is to triangulate around that member. Commonly, a couple may triangulate in connection with a mutual projection of a parental figure or a family ghost who can't talk for himself and is therefore subject to unlimited uncorrectable distortions. In Edward Albee's play *Who's Afraid of Virginia Woolf*, the couple tend to triangulate around a shared delusional child. An infant, being easily subjected to manipulation and distortions of its communications, can be grown almost totally ignored while the parents triangulate. (Bear in mind that what is ignored is not the topic of the infant. Indeed, both parents may be obsessed with it; but the human responses and spontaneous productions are missed in a cloud of discussion, argument, or commiserations between the parents.)

As the third member approaches total inoperability, he or she needs more and more to fuse, and one member of the primary pair may fuse with him or her, in which case the other member of the primary pair becomes insulated. In the case of parents, the less they tend to manipulate the child, the more the child will have a life and voice of its own. By the same token, the more autonomous the child, the more it becomes able to speak for itself and the less possible it is for the parents to shut it out. It is difficult to triangulate around an individual who demands personal recognition. If this occurs, the parents must deal with each other as individuals, conflict surfaces, and now the possibility develops that the couple will be insulated. This is dangerous for the child and explains why the child often appears to demand to be triangulated. It also explains why trouble in marriages commonly occurs around the times when children go from infancy to childhood, childhood to adolescence and, most frequently, when offspring leave home. It should be evident that although this discussion uses the so-called child-centered family as an example, the "primary pair"

Figure 2.2

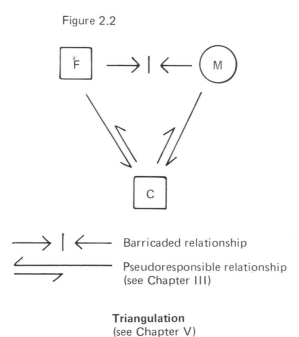

→ | ←     Barricaded relationship

Pseudoresponsible relationship
(see Chapter III)

**Triangulation**
(see Chapter V)

could be a parent and child, and the other parent could be triangulated. In this situation, it would be a parent-child relationship that was either in continuous conflict or nearly insulated, while the other parent-child relationship could tend to fuse (see Figure 2.3).

The major point I wish to make here is that fusion in one part of the system implies insulation from another part of the system. If the insulation is not within the family, it is between the family and the social systems around it. On the other hand, relatedness implies the sustainment of individuality. To the extent that one is forced to deal with the rest of the world, one cannot be fusing with one's neighbor. In fact, the way one maintains wholeness or selfhood is by constantly being aware of who one is in relation to the world while dealing with another. It is in this sense that I mean that there is no such thing as a pure twosome. Such a relationship could only become immediately a onesome — as segregation and centralization progress, one member of the dyad must become dominant and the other must become subordinate or independent, eventuating in fusion or insulation. It is only by being strongly related and connected to our emotional headquarters that we remain individuals. That which comprises our identity is not a lump, but an ever-fluid total picture of ourselves in relation to our parents and siblings, our spouses, and our children. It is not just the personality of a significant other that we internalize, but a prehension of the simultaneous interrelationships

Figure 2.3

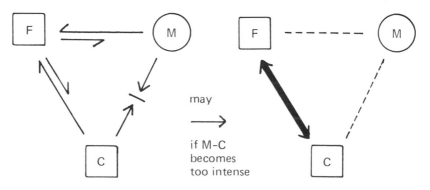

Triangulation                    Fusion and Insulation

of all significant others with our own belief and affect system. This would include the assignment of a rank order to significant others and would necessitate clearly distinguishing them from the rest of the world. Thus, the old teaser, "who would you save from drowning, your mother or Einstein?" should have a definite answer from a well-differentiated person. Such individuals do not isolate themselves, but rather, they make for strong families.

Good therapists, especially in treating couples and families, place great emphasis on "different-ness" (14), on recognizing it, respecting it, and dealing with it as important to the good functioning of a family. Correspondingly, von Bertalanffy states that "biological individuality does not exist, but only progressive individualization in evolution and development resulting from progressive centralization.... An individual is to be defined as a centered system" (15). A family, too, exists only insofar as it is centered and, as Nathan W. Ackerman has emphasized, a family without a strong identity is bound to be dysfunctional. It is important for those of us who tend to look primarily at pathology to bear in mind that the tendency toward fusion may have once been well-functioning leadership, and that insulation is specialization and individuality gone amok.

We therefore find that what is true of life is true of families: namely, that those processes necessary for growth, creativity, and continued good functioning also must eventuate in disintegration: Death begins with life. Less poetically, the twin processes of joining and separating, closing and distancing, fusing and insulating are not simply responses to the stimuli (concrete or symbolic) of hunger, sex, or aggression, but are intrinsic to human existence as a social animal; that is to say, as a part of an open hierarchial system.

## Other Principles of General System Theory and Family Counterparts

Living systems tend to approach a *stationary state* as an expression of the so-called principle of minimum effect. Any change in any variable at this point tends to be met by an

Figure 2.4

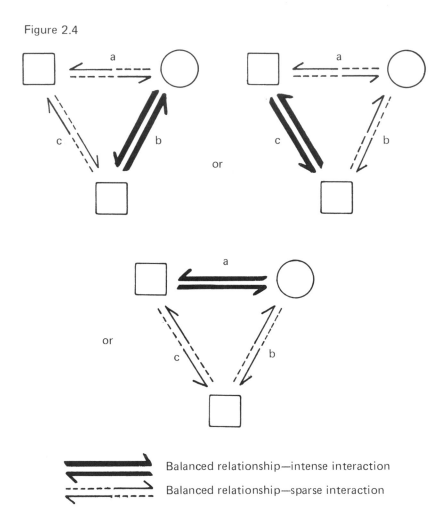

Balanced relationship—intense interaction

Balanced relationship—sparse interaction

$a + b + c \cong K$ **(sum of all interactions approximately constant)**
Where a, b, . . .is the quantity of interaction

Whenever one relationship of a threesome increases in intensity, there is a compensating decrease in intensity within the other two relationships.

opposing change such that the overall state of the system remains the same. The change in any variable occurs as a result of input from below or above (subsystem or suprasystem). If specific limits of input are exceeded, the steady state can no longer be maintained, and a change in state occurs. This means that either the system develops a new structure and process or it is destroyed.

Generally, the opposing changes that maintain steady states are governed by complex feedback mechanisms. We recognize here the well-known phenomenon of homestasis or "resistance" to change in a family. No sooner does a parental couple stop "scapegoating" a child, for example, than the child asks for it, even demands it. The moment a therapist gets some communication going between a distant couple, a third member breaks it up. When a pursuer stops pursuing a distancer, the distancer may become a pursuer. An especially interesting example is when one member of a threesome distances from the other two, the other two tend to become closer; conversely, when the distant member tends to get closer to either of the other two, the other two tend to move apart. Thus, a generality can be made that the total interaction of the three relationships tends to remain constant[2] (see Figure 2.4). This principle is used intuitively by some therapists when they try to increase

Figure 2.4 (continued)

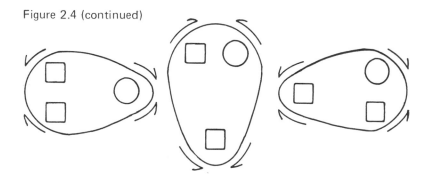

**The "Rubber-Band" Theory**

A distancing member of a threesome pulls the other two together. A decrease in distance of two members results in the distancing of the third.

[2]Sometimes known as Fogarty's "rubber-band" theory (16) as stretched by Ackerman.

interaction between child and father, for instance, to loosen the binding between mother and child (17).

The principle of *equifinality* separates the living from the dead. Hans Driesch's little sea urchin embryo proved it knew more than all the sages of its time when it blithely went on to develop into a whole animal after being halved. No more could Newtonian thinking claim to be capable of explaining all phenomena. It is now known that all living systems and some open nonliving systems can and will approach the same steady state (for a given type of system), starting from different conditions and utilizing different processess — different ingredients can still produce the same cake, even with different baking methods. The whole, then, is radically different from the sum of its parts, and its behavior can only be understood by the interrelatedness of its parts.

It is the patterns of interaction that determine the final state and, moreover, living systems undergo stepwise progressions toward a final state, each one being a steady state of higher organization than the previous one. This principle has been called *anamorphosis* and has the potential of explaining evolution, development, and creativity, all beyond the realm of the concepts of homeostasis and equilibrium. (Instinctual drives can never account for curiosity, for example.) Karl A. Menninger (18) recognized the importance of this principle with his introduction of the term *heterostasis* to describe the tendency to shift intrapsychic states. Arieti (19) points out that equifinality means that "initial conditions, although very important, do not constitute the only factor involved in the development of a normal or abnormal psyche." And again, "psychopathological conditions too, are states of high improbability which are maintained by negative psychological entropy coming from outside the system." Although *psychological entropy* is a contradiction in terms, I agree that the maintenance of the highly organized steady states we call mental illness depends upon adequate input from "outside the system," the most important aspect of which is generally the suprasystem or family. Remember, too, that negative entropy is information that is transmitted by communication.

## A Brief Clinical Illustration

Let us see, now, how equifinality and its associated concepts manifest themselves in family process. In the example of the overclose mother and child and distant father, mother may appear to be most desirous of having father and son get together, and particularly, of having father assume more responsibility; but no sooner does he move in this direction than she finds a million occasions to sabotage. A therapist working with this family might use various techniques at this point to enjoin mother from "forgetting" to relinquish control. Finally, when mother forgets to forget, father remembers to forget to assume control, and the earnest therapist goes to work on father's forgettory. Now the father forgets to remember to forget responsibility and the child promptly goes haywire, raging at father and demanding attention from mother. Everyone now appears to have a stake in keeping mother and son overclose and father distant. Thus far, we may say that homeostatic mechanisms are at work, homologous with those named by Cannon,[3] in that they are governed by preexisting processes of the system components (in this case, psychodynamics).

But such principles cannot explain subsequent events. A therapist who is psychoanalytically oriented may elect to "analyze out" mother's guilty reaction formation and fear of loss of control that help her to be such an "overprotective, overnurturing" parent. Or, the therapist may elect to work on father's castration fears, feelings of inadequacy, impounded rage, and all else that leads him to prefer a distant, passive position. Or, the separation anxieties and competitive conflicts of the son may be therapeutized while the parents are coached. Or, even more likely in this sophisticated age, some combination of all three approaches will be attempted, with emphasis on the interlocking pathology of the parents. If unsuccessful, it is chalked up to too much resistance of one sort or another. If successful, it is attributed to good interpretations with correct timing.

[3]It is instructive to read Walter B. Cannon's classic, *Wisdom of the Body* and discover what a great organismic and social systems thinker he was.

What one often misses, however, especially without long-term follow-up, is what I find to be a frequent happening: namely, that all is changed but all remains the same. Mother, losing her guilty fear, begins to encourage acting out or to demand gratification from the son. The son, losing his anxiety, begins to rebel, continuously criticizes mother and becomes competitively involved in peer groups. Father asserts himself by establishing more of a life for himself outside the home over wife's objections. His major interaction with son is commiserating about mother. In later family consultation all family members report they have gained a lot from therapy; but somehow, things aren't working. The child is failing in school, the marriage is on the rocks, and everyone wonders why, vaguely, the achieved insight has not made them happier. The analysis has worked. Their "personalities" are different. The family state is exactly the same as before: overclose mother and son relative to a distant father. The mother and son have tended to exchange functions with regard to the family system. The family is now more governed by the son than by mother[4] (Figure 2.5).

A therapist who is anti-analytic (which means calling oneself any number of things but conceiving of oneself as modern, free of old-fashioned rigidity and, in general, "having the word") will try in some fashion to rearrange the family. Such a therapist may work on communications and try to change patterns of sequences of interaction; may educate the family about triangles and coach them to avoid same; may get each individual to differentiate himself in his extended family; may become a lovable member of the family and use personal good offices to get the family to carry out certain tasks calculated to open up emotional give-and-take; may change intrapsychic conflict into resolvable interpersonal conflict. If the therapist hits the right paradoxical injunction or is intellectually convincing or becomes indispensable enough, father may be induced to give mother a holiday and, usually, the child's symptoms (such as school phobia) abate—whereupon a cure is hailed

---

[4]This is actually a shift from mother being the intermediary to mother being excluded. See Chapter V for more detailed description of various triangulation patterns.

(often in much shorter time than the child analyst takes). This kind of intervention is often so powerful that it is a make-or-break situation; that is, if the family cannot move with the therapist, the major alternative is to quit treatment, and the therapist shrugs and says "they just wouldn't see it my way and I have too much to do and too many people who are willing to be helped to knock myself out about this kind of situation."

What some therapists rarely see, as I do, a few years later, are those families who have gotten rearranged only to have a new outbreak of trouble in a new form. Mother has become liberated and is either having an affair, completely involved in community, or absorbed with women's consciousness. Father and son play tennis together, go on trips, and are constantly bickering about new-generation ideas, drugs (which the boy uses over father's impotent objections and without conceal-ment), and school (which the boy is failing). Again, the mar-riage is on the rocks and there is a distant parent and an

Figure 2.5

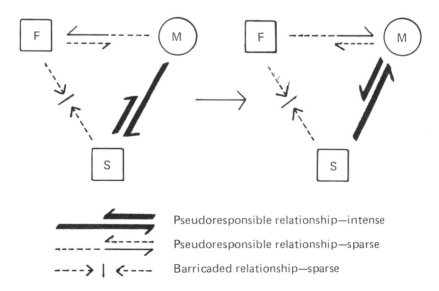

Pseudoresponsible relationship—intense

Pseudoresponsible relationship—sparse

Barricaded relationship—sparse

**Family pattern remains the same.**

Father and son take on pseudoresponsible attitudes toward mother.

overclose parent and child. The mother has usurped father's place in the system; the father occupies the son's place and the son does what mother did (see Figure 2.6).

The interesting thing about these last two examples is that there have been definite, often dramatic, changes in individual behavior (father has become quick-tempered and flamboyant; mother, cool and self-assured; son, defiant and adventurous), while the system reaches the same dysfunctional state. This is not simple homeostasis, and it cannot be explained on the basis of preexisting processes (psychodynamic or otherwise) in the individual. Rather, it says that the organization of the family follows its own principles, and that the individual may have to change radically to follow this powerful canon. Anyone who has ever tried to change his own behavior within his own family system knows the power whereof I speak; it is much more than the obstructionism or sabotaging of a few individuals.

## Some Consequences of Using General System Principles with Families

I say, therefore, that families qualify eminently for the designation "system" in the formal sense of the word, and that there is much to be learned by family therapists from what is

Figure 2.6

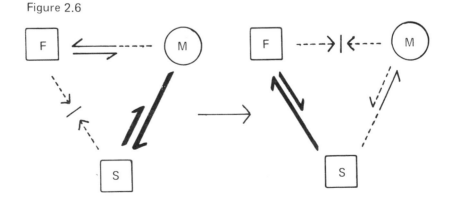

**Family pattern remains the same.**

All three relationships change in quality and/or intensity.

already known about systems. The above example, for instance, shows us that we may do our patients or clients a disservice when we attribute their resistance to unconscious motivations or even to family homeostasis. On the other hand, what appears to be family willingness to make changes may be a change of form only, and not substance. We need to be constantly refining our view of family process and to be vigilant about taking changes in individual process to be indicative of change in family process. Individual process is the *content* of family process.

Another assumption that family therapists frequently make is that "fits" between individual behavioral patterns (and, particularly, dysfunctional behavioral patterns) occur due to unconscious matching of couples. Underlying this assumption is the theory that individual dynamics are fixed long before marriage and determine family patterns. Rather, it may be (and often is, in my opinion) the magnificent adaptability of the individual at work when we see his inner conflicts meshing beautifully with the family system. More and more, I tend to believe my patients when they tell me, "George wasn't that way at all when I married him."

Further, the example highlights what we already know: that a sadomasochistic marriage is no better or worse than a masochistosadistic marriage, and that a true reversal of interaction and psychodynamics can happen before our eyes. It suggests that dealing with only a couple can be haphazard and incomplete. It warns us that the report that an individual feels improved may be misleading. It makes us beware of fast cures and demand long-term follow-up. Most importantly, such examples point to the general criteria of health.

At the beginning of this discussion, I said that we might arrive at some predictive tools, and I believe we have. It is almost certain that if the degree of interaction of one relationship is increased (becomes closer) then a compensatory decrease will occur in at least one other relationship. It can also be safely predicted that in a family with dysfunctional members, if the quality of their relationships within the family do not improve, the functioning of these members does not improve. They may report feeling better or liking themselves better, yet their relationships are not working or their jobs aren't satisfactory or they are not getting what they want out of life.

Moreover, if the interaction patterns simply change from one set of relationships to another without a change in the *general* state or balance of the family, the family and the individuals in it will remain dysfunctional. The family will fail to nourish and provide the context for growth.

## Criteria of Health for Families

The criteria of health I therefore consider to be

1. that all relationships in a family be balanced with respect to responsibility, and

2. that the amount of personal interaction of each relationship in the family be approximately the same (see Figure 2.7).

These two criteria need some elaboration.

The term *balanced* is used here with respect to responsibility, to indicate a mutual, cooperative give-and-take relationship that is enhancing for both individuals simultaneously. In such a relationship, each individual initiates interaction regarding his or her own needs and responds adequately to the other's initiations regarding the other's needs. This does not imply that A will initiate as *often* nor make as *many* responses as B, but rather that A and B each will initiate appropriately according to his own needs and will respond when called upon. Thus, although a colicky infant may do most of the initiating of interaction with mother (who does most of the responding), when mother out of her own need at a quiet moment tries to elicit a smile or look, the infant is as responsive to her as she was to it. Each is taking responsibility for self and is a leader or trigger with regard to interaction gratifying his or her own needs, and yet each is governed by the other with regard to the other's needs. Segregation has proceeded far enough to distinguish one's needs from the other and centralization has proceeded far enough to be able to rely on the other.

This is to be contrasted with what I call *pseudoresponsible relationships*. The same mother and child, for example, could have a relationship completely centralized around mother. The mother would try to anticipate all the baby's needs, initiating all interaction so that the infant takes no responsibility for self and simply responds to mother. This phenomenon has been observed by many authors and has been given various names, among them, skewered (20) and pseudomutual (21).

At bottom of the balanced relationship is a shared attitude or point of view: I am willing to be at cause in the matter of whether or not my needs are gratified in this relationship; I am responsible. In such a relationship there is no blaming; only a mutual willingness to make it work.

The second criterion of health in a family means that, although there are always fluctuations and differences in degrees of intensity from one relationship to another, over time it averages out. For any given relationship, it is equally probable

Figure 2.7

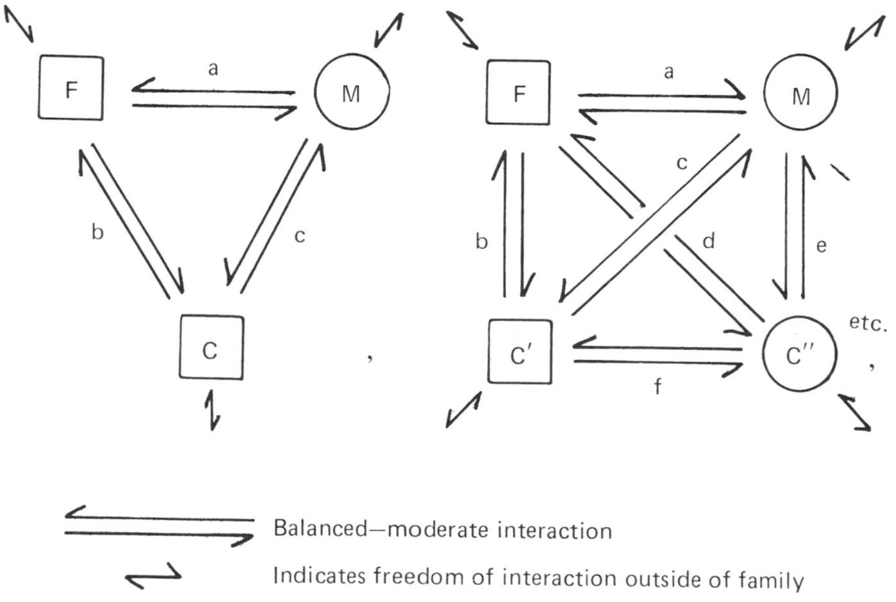

Balanced—moderate interaction

Indicates freedom of interaction outside of family

**The Healthy Family**

$a \cong b \cong c \cong d \cong e$ ... etc. (amount of interaction same)

The healthy family is balanced with respect to responsibility and all relationships are approximately the same with respect to amount of *personal* interaction.

to become more or less intense in the long run. Each relationship is therefore equally mobile (free to distance or close). In order for this to be so, each individual must be able to interact *outside* the family system as well. Note very importantly that *intensity* refers to amount of personal interaction. *Personal* is defined as the conveyance of affect or belief regarding the relationship to the other in such a way as to allow for the other to respond in kind. Thus it is possible for a father away at work to have just as much personal interaction with baby during the time he is at home as mother has with baby all day.

## Final Considerations

Viewing people as part of a system may seem to some readers like relegating human beings to the position of cog on a gear. Quite the contrary is true, as has been amply demonstrated by von Bertalanffy in *Robots, Men and Minds* (22). The first thing I point out to people in therapy is that if they are truly part of a system, the most efficient way to change it is to change their own behavior in the system. Everyone must shift if one person shifts. This undercuts all blaming and alibi-making and gives each person the opportunity to take as much responsibility as he or she is willing to have. Like so many either – or issues, that of free will versus determinism appears to be a false one. One may make many choices regarding one's behavior within the limitations set by the rules of one's inner system; all these choices will affect the larger system of which one is a part, and this, in turn, will affect oneself. The trick is to learn what changes produce desirable corresponding changes in the larger system, which in turn is governed by its own canon, within which there may be much variation.

Let us remember that the greatest value of general system theory is that it offers us a point of view that we can use when observing the phenomena in which we are interested. It finds no data for us, nor does it presume to tell us the specific processes involved in any given system. It is for us dealing with families to do this job and to constantly revise and refine our findings.

Subsequent chapters will elaborate upon the family processes just described, and the canon we arrive at will be used to illuminate some of the clinical work of well-known therapists and some common clinical phenomena.

# References

1. Menninger, Karl A., Mayman, Martin, and, Pruyser, Paul, *The Vital Balance,* (New York: Viking, 1963).

2. von Bertalanffy, Ludwig, "General System Theory and Psychiatry," in Sylvano E. Arieti (ed.), *American Handbook of Psychiatry,* vol. 3 (New York: Basic Books, 1967).

3. Grinker, Roy Sr., (ed.), *Toward a Unified Theory of Human Behavior* (New York: Basic Books, 1967).

4. Gray, William, Duhl, Frederick J., and, Rizzo, Nicholas D., (eds.), *General Systems Theory and Psychiatry* (Boston: Little, Brown, 1969).

5. Durkin, Helen E. "Analytic Group Therapy and General Systems Theory," in Sager, Clifford J. and Kaplan, Helen S. (eds.), *Progress in Group and Family Therapy* (New York: Brunner/Mazel, 1972), 9-17.

6. von Bertalanffy, Ludwig, *General System Theory* (New York: Braziller, 1968), 33, 55.

7. Campbell, D.T., "Common Fate, Similarity and Other Indices of the Status of Aggregates of Persons as Social Entities, *Behavioral Science,* 3 (1958), 14.

8. Ashby, W. Ross, "Principles of the Self-Organizing System," in von Foerster, H., Zipf, G.W., (eds.), *Principles of Self-Organization* (New York: Pergamon, 1962), 255-257, 266.

9. Miller, James G., "Living Systems: Basic Concepts," in Gray et al., *General Systems Theory and Psychiatry,* 66.

10. Ackerman, Nathan W., *The Psychodynamics of Family Life* (New York: Basic Books, 1958), 19.

11. *Ibid.,* 52-67.

12. Bowen, Murray, "The Theory and Practice of Psychotherapy," in Philip J. Guerin, Jr. (ed.), *Family Therapy: Theory and Practice* (New York: Gardner, 1976), 66.

13. Wynne, Lyman C., Ryckoff, Irving M., Day, Juliana, and Hirsch, Stanley I., "Pseudomutuality in the Family Relations of Schizophrenics," *Psychiatry,* (1958), 205, 220.

14. Satir, Virginia, V., *Conjoint Family Therapy* (Palo Alto, California: Science and Behavior Books, 1964).

15. von Bertalanffy, *General System Theory*, 73.

16. Fogarty, Thomas P. personal communication.

17. Haley, Jay, and Barragan, Mariano A., "A Modern 'Little Hans,'" Videotape, Philadelphia Child Guidance Clinic, n.d.

18. Menninger, Karl A., "Designated Discussion," in Gray et al. *General Systems Theory and Psychiatry*, 47.

19. Arieti, *American Handbook of Psychiatry*, 49.

20. Lidz, Theodore, *The Origin and Therapy of Schizophrenic Disorders* (New York: Basic Books, 1973).

21. Wynne, Lyman C., et al., "Pseudomutuality in the Family Relations of Schizophrenics,"

22. von Bertalanffy, Ludwig, *Robots, Man and Minds* (New York: Braziller, 1967).

**III**
# THE
# THREESOME

**m**any years ago, at a conference concerning the possible pathological effects of children upon a marriage, Nathan W. Ackerman, in a remarkable discussion, pointed out the stabilizing, healing, and growth-promoting influences of children (1). Among the factors he cited were the extension of meaning of the family beyond sex and marriage, enabling the individual to transcend self in a creative function; the binding of parents far beyond the relatively transitory binding of sexuality; the bridging between old and new; the linking of the family with the world at large; the possibility of finding immortality in an ongoing family identity; the reinforcement of parental conscience; the challenge to rise to the child's idealization of the parent; and, finally, the stimulus of the child's critical protests. In the same discussion, it was reported that the attempt of psychiatric residents or analytic students to predict the type of parents a child might have from the evaluation of the child or, conversely, to predict the kind of child a parental pair might have after interviewing them, often proved totally unreliable. The unreliability appeared to be due, in part, to the tendency to base the judgment on a concept of a one-to-one emotional interchange between the child and the parent. Further:

> This cannot be done. It is scientifically incorrect. The child adapts emotionally to the family group as a unity, not exclusively to one or the other parent as individual. One cannot formulate the emotional interchange between parent and child to the exclusion of a third party, and the family as a whole. This never occurs in nature and therefore the question is posed in a false way. There is always a third person, and more.... Whenever in life a twosome appears to exclude the influence and participation of the third person, if one closely examines the emotional interchange of the pair, one finds there is a barricading within the pair. Sooner or later, the one shuts out the other. The twosome is distorted regressively into a onesome. The true unit of relationships is a threesome.

If we expand the meaning of "shuts out" to a general denial of the other as an individual, this can be accomplished in three ways. One can distance to the point of cutting off the other altogether. One can close in upon the other to the point of invasion or engulfment, disqualifying the other's being with preoccupation with self or overwhelming the other with projections. Finally, one can appear to relate to the other, but only by communicating about a third party or thing, refusing to allow any direct, personal exchanges. These three processes correspond to the terms insulation, fusion, and triangulation, introduced in the previous chapter.

## Attributes of a Threesome

A twosome is inherently unstable. A relationship that is mutual and cooperative, in which each person accepts full responsibility for the relationship, invites participation by others and quickly becomes at least a threesome. In a threesome, there are three distinct, simultaneously interacting, give-and-take, mutal, person-to-person relationships. This is not a simple sum of three; rather, the nature of the operation depends on the total organization. In human terms, the simultaneity of the relationships means each is privy to the others and therefore affected by them. Also, the operation of each individual with respect to the other two will hinge not only on the other two's operation with the individual but also on their relationship with each other. The third person can be said to couple the other two. (See the reference to Ashby's discussion of conditionality in Chapter II.)

## Well Functioning and Impaired Functioning in a Threesome

Implicit in the notion of the threesome as an efficiently functioning unit is the maintenance of clear lines of communication and affect exchange. What is between father and child is not the same thing as what is between mother and child or between mother and father, and each member must be assured the unhampered opportunity to respond freely to each of the other two. Conversely, no member speaks for another to the third. (This does not mean that one cannot be a spokesperson to others outside the threesome.) Note that the moment one member assumes the role of mouthpiece, such as mother defending a defiant boy to father, this opens up the possibility of endless futile debate and actually prevents the issue at hand from being handled effectively. If the parents get into a discussion about the child, the child is shut out and the parents have stopped relating to each other in a direct fashion (See Figure 3.1). At this point, the parents can continue to be deadlocked, alternating intense and sparse interaction; or one of the parents can give way and distance toward insulation while the other parent tends to fuse with the child (See Figure 3.2). Each one of these shifts in steady states is a step toward higher organization, the end point of which would be total fusion —

that is, completely rigid coupling of all entities. At this point, all entities would merge into an individual organism.

Clinically, some families approach this state, and one is hard put to distinguish one point of view from another or even to discern who is who. More often, mother and father will indulge in endless debate about parenting; mother and son will commiserate about the tyrannical father, and/or father and son can fight about the respect due or not due mother (See Figure 3.3). In all instances, no one is relating directly to anyone else and the communications are ineffectual. In order to prevent this from becoming a predominant pattern, each individual must take responsibility for self vis-à-vis all other individuals in the family. This means speaking for oneself, not speaking for others, not condoning (let alone requesting) that others speak for oneself, and refusing to allow another to speak

Figure 3.1

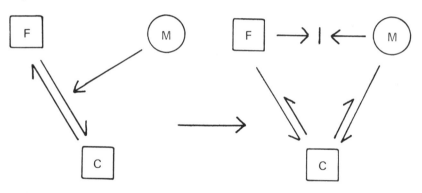

Interruption of father-child
relationship by mother.

Father-mother relationship
is now *about* child and the child
is partly shutout.

Dysfunctional communication (misdirected or interruption)

Pseudoresponsible relationship (imbalanced)

Barricaded relationship

to oneself for a third party. Note that such behavior demands openness and results in issues being brought up directly, rather than being suppressed. To prevent the fusion type of dysfunction in a threesome requires that a third person must interact with the first two as much as they interact with each other.

Figure 3.2

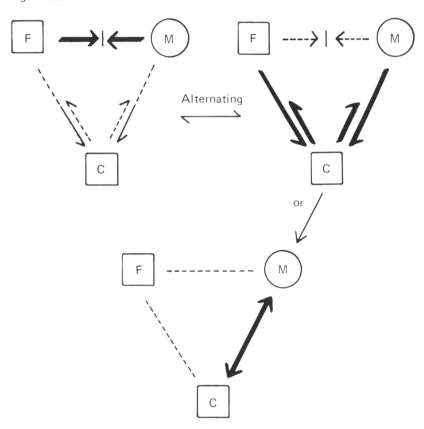

Intense conflict between parents effectively shuts out child. Barricaded distance between parents results in both intensifying attempts to take responsibility for the child (oversolicitousness or overdisciplining, for example). If one parent eventually monopolizes the child, near–fusion occurs and the other parent is insulated.

*Rules for Optimum Functioning*

Clinical considerations, therefore, lead us to the following rules of thumb for optimum functioning: (1) Each relationship in a family must be distinct from the others and each person in a relationship must relate directly to the other for effective conflict resolution and task completion; (2) there must not be too much closeness or too much distance in any one relationship, so that no two individuals become entangled and no one gets shut out. These two rules are concrete descriptions of the more abstract criteria for health arrived at in Chapter II.

Figure 3.3

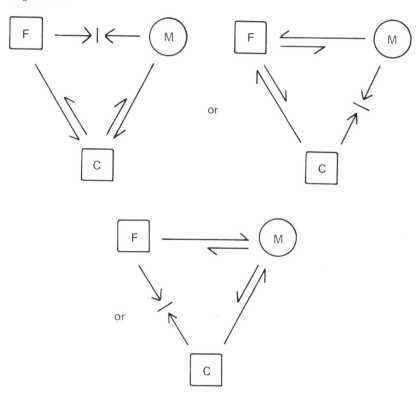

Any pair of a threesome may relate by banding against, idolizing or fighting over the third member. One pair may do this predominantly or all three may take turns.

# The Twosome and the Threesome Compared

The argument raised by some is that the dyad is the basic relationship, and this question ought to be examined. If we consider "systems" only in mechanistic terms (for example, servo regulators and positive loops), we could call a couple a system. The moment we begin to study families *per se*, however, we see that the circular casuality that does occur between pairs cannot, even by summation, satisfactorily account for family behavior. We must deal with principles of growth, competition, wholeness, and organization. Two entities cannot be organized without a variable condition set down by a third that provides some constraint, a coupling effect. Otherwise, they would be independent variables or so rigidly coupled as to be locked in — that is, cogs.

Clinically, I would submit that a true one-to-one relationship does not exist. In the first place, "no man is an island;" one's identity is shaped by an ongoing dialectic (what might better be termed multilectic) with significant others (2). Being personal, then, means in some way to call into play these significant others. In the second place, to sustain a relationship between two people without others is extremely difficult, if not impossible. On the sociological level, childless marriages require a larger context in which to work; otherwise, they often become triangulated about lovers, extended family, or a work network. On the level of relationship, to carry on a person-to-person conversation for more than a few minutes is rare if we define such a conversation as consisting of statements about self (feelings or beliefs) vis-à-vis the other conveyed to the other in such a way that the other can respond in kind. What generally happens is that at the first sign of distancing (such as an expression of disinterest or boredom) or closure (such as direct anger or affection) and the attendant anxiety, there is an attempt to triangulate. Challenge any well-functioning couple to go to a crowded restaurant with poor service, sit at a small table face to face, and see how long they can engage one another without getting angry at the waiter, commiserating with the waiter or one attacking and the the other defending the waiter (3). While there is nothing intrinsically wrong with talking about the waiter, in this instance it is done to avoid completing a personal communication.

To be fully expressive in a relationship requires that one be clear that he or she is whole and sufficient without the other. This occurs regularly and only, in my experience, in those individuals whose percepts of their original family change form childhood distortions (positive or negative) to a clear view of them as ordinary people. Simultaneously, with the separating out and loss of distortion, there occurs a sense of belonging to one's family of origin. I am saying that the ability to relate and continue to respond as a whole person to another, to maintain oneself and neither fuse nor insulate nor be forced to triangulate, requires a strong and well-defined historical bond to significant others. In fact, I would say that the essence of any psychotherapy is the attempt to tighten, rework, or form such bonds. What is labeled operationally, then, as "person-to-person" is actually the joining of two systems, and one-to-one is a meeting of at least two threesomes, each complete in itself (Figure 3.4).

In such an ideal relationship, neither person needs to parentify nor infantilize the other. They meet as peers and recognize in each other a uniqueness that can combine with their

Figure 3.4

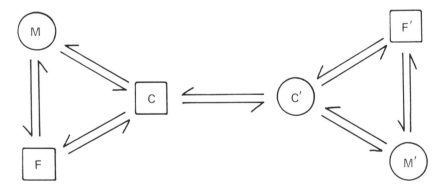

Well-functioning threesomes allow and encourage members to relate to outsiders. When two individuals form a balanced relationship, the original threesome is included.

own to form something new. Moreover, there is generally a creative move to share ideas, to build something, to form a team, to raise children. Well-functioning couples have goals that are larger than their relationship. This tendency may be viewed as a specific instance of the tendency of living systems to shift toward states of higher organization, or to feed on negentropy, as Schroedinger (4) put it. This is no mystery, and no *élan vital* is required to explain it; having been spawned and grown in a threesome, humans tend to develop threesomes.

## Family-Seeking Behavior or the Need for a Threesome

Familial-seeking behavior, as I call it, is very powerful. Those individuals who try to insulate themselves from their families of origin are engaging in a desperate act of self-assertion—the only way they can achieve some degree of autonomy. These people, having lost the opportunity to become integrated into their family in a growth-enhancing manner, will tend to make a whole family out of another individual, be doomed to disappointment, and go through cycle after cycle of fusion and insulation. An interesting discussion of such individuals may be found in Scheflen's paper on regressive onesomes (5). So-called transference phenomena that occur in the analyst's office are examples of the need to work out filial relationships; but these are generally only understood as a distortion of reality by repetition of the past, rather than as primarily a seeking for closeness. Resistance, on the other hand, is a tendency to distance. Often, the analysand seeks both individuality and relationship through indentity within a family, as manifested by fantasizing about the analyst's spouse and children as well as by shifting back and forth from maternal to paternal transference.

## *The Subordination of Character to Family Adaptation*

The term transference has also been loosely applied to small-group behavior and family interaction, where, for example, it is interpreted that the wife is treating her husband as if he were her father while the husband is "making" the wife into his mother. Of course, if one finds a partner with dovetailing habits, as one often does, repetitions of past child-parent patterns will be seen. But it also happens that spouses don't exactly match psychologically, and the mode of interaction may then be determined largely by the past behavior patterns of one spouse, with the other learning new patterns. Thus, when two spoiled brats meet, one may, for the first time, take on the role of the doting parent. A big brother, used to being the caretaker, may become the baby, or a little sister may become overadequate. I use this capability at times by teaching a burden-assuming spouse to behave irresponsibly in order to give room for the other spouse to become more responsible.

Of course, this can be partially explained by the fact that many character traits are one side of a coin (uncharitably called reaction formation), but circumstances such as illness or financial disaster may render old patterns of relating unusable and demand new ones from the whole family. We may then see new character traits emerge that are not at all opposite of old ones. When that occurs, attempts to equate current behavioral patterns with those from a family of origin are refuted by the patient; and one can either believe that the patient is hiding the truth to frustrate the theory or conclude that familial-seeking behavior is more fundamental to the human organism than even the individual's original family role. In my view, people will go through major personality and character changes in order to adapt to a family.

## *The Threesome is a Context for the Expression of Two Sides of Mankind*

Koestler has made an excellent case for the twin tendencies to become a part of a whole (self-transcend) and to individuate (self-assert) being both inherent in the human organism structure (6). As the human organism develops, the individual's psychic apparatus or inner system organizes into self-regulating, interacting structures with ever-increasing centralization and specialization of parts, a process that eventuates in more and more indivisibility or individuality. (See the discussion of progressive centraization in Chapter II.) Just so, the family in time organizes, and its members with respect to it become more and more specialized and more and more reliant on other members for functions complementary to their own. In this sense, humans become progressively more incomplete parts of a whole. The development of an individual follows that of the species. As primitive humans were able to move their culture in many directions, so the infant has tremendous versatility and many potentials. Each stage of development, however, seems to close the door to previous stages, and the more skilled one becomes, the fewer options one has for future goals. With respect to inner self, one becomes more unified; with respect to social matrix, one becomes more a fragment.

The expression of this duality of the human being is naturally achieved in the context of the parent-child threesome. One asserts oneself as mate, and one transcends oneself as parent. The creation of a new system out of the merger of two old ones allows for the perfect balance of the two faces of human endeavor. The child is important, for transcendence of oneself with a mate often becomes perverted into a self-sacrifice or infantilization of the other, which, if sustained, in turn means the loss of self for each person. With a child, who is not yet a whole person, one can regulate without being destructive, and it is only the child who can, by identification, take true personal pride in another's accomplishments. I am not saying that a mate cannot be proud of a mate, but if this is used as a substitute for one's own accomplishments, it must lead to loss of self-esteem and humiliation. For a child, however, it is growth-enhancing for self-esteem to derive from a parent. Moreover, as a parent, one can truly allow the child to partake of all one has or is without being diminished thereby and can take all the creative pride in the child's growth that one wishes without taking away from the child.

# The Dangers of Twosomeness

Consenting adults trying to achieve this kind of relationship often (after the honeymoon) become lopsided in power distribution, mimic a child-parent relationship, and lose mutuality. The pseudoparent becomes burdened and the pseudochild becomes humiliated. At the same time, each requires the other for completion. Then master becomes slave to the slave, and slave becomes master to the master. The resultant coercive binding eliminates emotional mobility and freedom of choice. Volition being no longer there, spontaneity and creativity cannot emerge. There is no newness, no growth, no life. The system is now closed and tending toward true equilibrium as opposed to a steady state. This system cannot admit an outsider; any input is necessarily disruptive. The balance is too tenuous and the danger of breakup is too great. Fusion, then, is a natural consequence of twosomeness, and couples who fuse tend to have great emotional outbursts with subsequent distance or insulation.

It should be made clear at this point that, although the discussion is centering about a male-female couple, the same descriptions can apply to any twosome, even when they are of different generations or the same sex (5). In a word, any two can fuse, and then the rest of the world must be shut out or the relationship will be torn apart. Conversely, the presence of a functioning third person prevents fusion and insulation.


*Can "Togetherness" Work?*


Why can't a twosome be all things to each other? Why must it be destructive? The point to remember is that either progressive segregation or progressive centralization, when carried to an end point, means the end of the system as such. The former results in an independence of parts that are no longer related, and the latter eventuates in a rigid interconnectedness, such that all parts are cogs, not individuals. This means that the altruistic joining, socializing (self-transcending) side of man can be just as destructive as the aggressive, competitive, individuating (self-assertive) side. Koestler (7) has pointed out in this connection that very little destructiveness has been perpetrated for self-aggrandizement as compared with the devastation wrought by zealots in the name of some holy cause. We have many ways of regulating the former and practically no way to handle the latter. Equally, in a family there are many ways of dealing with naked aggression; even children have ways of coping with parental terror, and these ways can be life-saving, at least, and often neutralizing. But that terrible need of humans to join, to belong, to create and leave behind more than themselves can frequently, when misdirected, unleash destructive operations that are almost impossible to control. Killing kindness can be irresistible. It is extremely difficult to deal with the parent whose self-sacrifice for the child is so great that there is nothing left of the child. This is particularly true because it is not simple hypocrisy that speaks, but a genuine need to subvert the self to the other. I refer you again to Koestler (8) for a description and explanation of this mechanism.

The point here is that we have been so obsessed with the dangers of self-aggrandizement that we have neglected the possible consequences of self-transcendency. Any self-transcendency that is carried to the obliteration of self is destructive for all. Yet the motivation appears benign, not only intellectually, but emotionally; the losing of self in the process of creation rings a bell in all of us. We can be horrified by or sympathetic to the self-immolater, but we are not programed to defend ourselves against this kind of person, although such a one can set off a holocaust. Another aspect is that the self-assertive tendency demands dominance or sole proprietorship, whereas the self-transcendent tendency must have another person to operate on. Thus a child who stays out of the way, for instance, might be left alone by an aggressive, competitive parent, but a self-sacrificing parent will not allow distance. It becomes impossible for the child to resist the parent who is convinced that all that he or she does is in the best interest of the child. The overprotection, the infantilization, the continual gratification set up a vicious cycle at the expense of individua-

tion and self-assertion. The resistance is always there in the
form of protest and attempts at independent action, but without support, such attempts stir great anxiety that cannot be
handled. An attempt to support independence by the other
parent would constitute disruption and be rejected by both
first parent and child. The longer this situation obtains, the
less the child can be alone and the more threatening learning
self-reliance becomes. Being unable to care for self is the *sine
qua non* of pathology in our society. This, it would seem to
me, is the ultimate consequence of insisting upon maintaining
twosomeness.

## What About Independence?

On the other hand, the person who learns to be more independent through self-defense against aggression, we con-
ceive of as able to function, although, in truth, such a person
may be just as crippled when it comes to being a member of
the human race. We generally do not regard people who manage to survive on their own as incapacitated. We may regard
them as dangerous. Those who only need to latch onto others,
we regard as weak, but harmless. This is obviously a cultural
prejudice that values individuality above all and therefore
labels dependence as sick and independence as healthy. The
prejudice is reinforced by our tendency to look at the intrapsychic (as we experience ourselves) rather than at the interpersonal. In other words, those individuals who have "coped"
with open aggression may simply look healthier to our preju-
diced eye. My guess is that on close examination, if they are
found to be truly healthier (that is, better able to relate, as well
as to maintain themselves), it is not because they have cut
themselves off from their family of origin (as often happens),
but rather because in so doing they have been able to join, at
least partially, another family.

## Which is Worse?

The question of whether or not self-transcendency intrinsically has more destructive potential than self-assertion is
moot. One could say that the posing of such a question is an

anthropomorphization of a systems concept, and that such a notion is a reflection of the same individualistic prejudice, namely, that fusion is more evil than insulation. One could also argue that fusion requires at least two people, whereas insulation requires only one. The self-sacrificing parent must have a child. The aggressive, competitive parent wants not to join, and this frees the child. The answer is that this is an example of one-to-one thinking that distorts the actuality. The child never has to face the one situation or the other. If one parent tends to fuse with the child, it can only be that the other parent is distant from the child. If both parents are fusing with each other or insulating from one another, the child will not become a functioning person without outside help.

## The Threesome is a Condition for Well-Being

In any case, optimum functioning demands that human beings be both dependent and independent, part of an outer system and a unified whole with respect to a personal inner system. This needs to be achieved in the context of a threesome. Although spouses and friends may mother and father each other at times, they cannot sustain it simultaneously, but must take turns to some extent. Also, the quality must remain one of partiality or role-playing, so as to retain the freedom to regain the basic partnership. Husband and wife, for instance, can only maintain mutuality if the power distribution is equal and both are free to close or distance at will. Obligatoriness diminishes or at least makes questionable the love component. The parent-child relationship, on the other hand, is naturally lopsided with respect to power, yet mutuality can be maintained. This is because mutuality does not depend on absolute power but, rather, it relies on each person contributing to the relationship in accord with his or her capability. As Holt has expounded, the natural authority of an adult demands mutual recognition of the unequal power distribution in a child-adult relationship, and to pretend otherwise is dysfunctional (except in play) (9).

All the considerations of the foregoing discussion may be applied to other threesomes, such as couple and parent or couple and friend or couple and colleague. Childless couples who have fulfilling relationships maintain intimacy with others outside their marriage. Frequently, these relationships have a legitimate parent-child quality, such as teacher-student or employer-employee, and may be shared by the couple. Occasionally, the outside relationship may be to a cause or an organization.

The third relationship is not a guarantee of well-being. It is simply a necessary condition. It provides a matrix for the growth-promoting expression of all the natural tendencies of humanity, and humans demand all for fulfillment.

# Reference

1. Ackerman, Nathan W., Discussion of *The Effects of Children on Marriage,* by Theodore Lidz (Paper presented at A Conference on Psychoanalysis and Marriage, Yale University, New Haven, Conn., 1959).

2. Boszormenyi-Nagy, Ivan, "A Theory of Relationships: Experience and Transaction," in *Intensive Family Therapy,* Ivan Boszormenyi-Nagy and James L. Framo (eds.) (New York: Harper & Row, 1965), 35-41.

3. I am indebted to Thomas P. Fogarty for this cogent example.

4. Schroedinger, Erwin, *What is Life?* (New York: Macmillan, 1945), 72, 83.

5. Scheflen, Albert E., "Regressive One to One Relationships," *Psychiatric Quarterly, 34* (1960), 692-704.

6. Koestler, Arthur, *The Ghost in the Machine* (New York: Macmillan, 1976), 56-58.

7. *Ibid.,* 233-235.

8. *Ibid.,* 190-192, 242-243.

9. Holt, John C., *Freedom and Beyond* (New York: Dutton, 1972), 49-76.

CHAPTER **IV**

# FUSION AND
# INSULATION

**W**e have seen that the twin tendencies of human beings to join and to separate are expressions of one's being both a whole unto oneself and a part unto one's family. Developmentally, these two aspects unfold simultaneously, so that the more one becomes an integral part of the family, the more of a unified whole the inner system becomes. This "transformation from a more general and homogeneous to a more special and hetero-geneous condition" (1) is not peculiar to humans; on the con-trary, "wherever development occurs it proceeds from a state of relative... lack of differentiation to a state of increasing dif-ferentiation, articulation and hierarchic order" (2). The most oft-quoted example of this process of differentiation is taken from biology: the embryo's cells become progressively more integrated into organs as they become differentiated one from the other. Moreover – and this, also, is relevant to people sys-tems – at successive stages, there appear to be points of no return; that is, initially, any cell of the embryonic mass, if separated from its neighbors, can go on to subdivide, differentiate and form a whole individual, but once differentiation has occurred, ectodermal cells, for example, can only go on to differentiate further into the various derivatives of ectoderm.(There is some evidence, of late, that this can be reversed in the laboratory). Hierarchy is everywhere; phylogeny, culture, and psychosocial organization follow the same general patterns.

## Centralization and Differentiation

Koestler has coined the word *holon* (3) to denote that an entity within a hierarchical system is simultaneously a particle and a whole. An entity is something that can be examined in its own right and we commonly agree that among those entities of the psychosocial hierarchy that have discernible boundaries are people, families, and clans. All these are holons; simultaneously all display (a) differentiated wholeness with respect to their subsystem and (b) integrated partness with respect to their suprasystems.

As pointed out previously, to have integrated parts means necessarily to have centralization and differentiation. Loss of centralization or loss of differentiation means loss of organization and, hence, of function. Note that one cannot have differentiation without centralization and vice-versa; yet the end point of either as a process means the loss of the other. Once differentiation proceeds to the point of mechanization (that is, when each entity does its own thing irrespective of others), relatedness is lost, and there is no longer regulability, dominance, or centralization. Once centralization proceeds to the point of indivisibility of the system, the boundaries of the system's entities blur, and differentiation is lost. In the first instance, the holon becomes fragmented; in the second, it becomes a closed system. Both descriptions apply to multiple levels of the psychosocial hierarchy: to the psychic apparatus in the state labeled schizophrenic; to the psychotic family — Wynne's "rubber fence" (4) and Lidz's families that relate only in twos (5); and to malfunctioning networks — Speck and Attneave's collusions and loosening (6). All systems proceed toward fragmentation *and* closure. At the moment fragmentation and closure occur, organization is lost and the system ceases to exist as a system.


## *Psychosis and the Relation Between Inner and Outer Systems*

The unmeasurably small interval between having organization and not having it is the difference between life and death. It is for good reason that schizophrenic patients were called the "living dead"; for, like an excised heart in a perfusion bath, the individual apart from its hierarchy lives on yet does not live. Its parts operate without meaning; for living beings, there is no functioning without organization.

It is generally agreed that no single sign or symptom is pathognomonic of schizophrenia, and that the loss of integration of all mental operations is crucial. Yet this seems to be poorly understood. It is an attribute of systems that they either *are* or are *not*; there is no such thing as an almost system or a halfway system. If the words *schizophrenia* and *psychosis* have any operational meaning at all, they must signify *at least* that the person's mental operations are not functioning as a system at the time the terms are applied. Yet one talks of the continuum of mental illness and of borderline schizophrenia and process (or progressive) schizophrenia. The term *decompensation* often connotes a more or less gradual process of going from an organized to a disorganized state. Clinically, however, we may see instantaneous shifts from one state to the other, sometimes several in a single interview, and it is most common for floridly psychotic person admitted one night to hospital to be clear as a bell the next day (sometimes called "sealing over").

Only the principles of a system can account for these phenomena. As for the changes seen in so-called chronic psychosis, these are simply the gradual deterioration of individual mental functions once disorganization has occurred. The process of developing an overcentralized mental apparatus is also a time-dependent operation and can put one dangerously close to disorganization. This is the situation of some geniuses. Paul Morphy, the American chess marvel, is one such example who has been described in the literature (7).

If one considers the terms used to describe psychosis clinicially, there appears to be a lot of confusion: withdrawal, decathexis and going into a shell are apparent contradictions to loosening, failure of repression, and loss of ego boundaries. Again, such terms as sealing over and coming out of the shell used to describe recovery from psychosis also appear contradictory. Withdrawal, however, is an interpersonal phenomenon, whereas loosening of associations is intrapsychic. Both are part of what we term psychosis and they must both occur *only and always* together. It follows that if we can find ways to achieve inner organization, then relationships improve, and this statement is generally accepted. What holds equally true but is not generally accepted by people outside the family therapy movement is that improving the outer system or relationships must result in improved inner organization of the individual. (I hasten to add that I do not mean simply making friends, but rather, becoming integrated into a well-functioning kinship system as defined in Chapter III.) This is not an audacious statement; it simply is a tautological one. Only a well-functioning individual could be an integral part of a well-functioning kinship system and, in fact, would not be without one.

The complementarity of inner and outer systems enables us to describe and define dysfunction from either point of view, so long as we do not apply the specific canon of one system to the other, or forget *which* system we are observing *when*. Thus, psychosis can be viewed as the loss of relatedness, that is, a person's attainment of complete autonomy from significant others. As has been thoroughly expounded—by de Cusa, Fichte, Hegel, Buber, Freud, and recently, Boszormenyi-Nagy (8)—loss of relationships automatically means loss of self.

Looking more closely at the outer system in conjunction with individual psychosis, however, leads to interesting new views of psychosis. For example, both temporal and spatial considerations begin to be important, and one can ask When is psychosis? and Where is psychosis? as well as What is psychosis? A person who is psychotic to a psychiatrist may be perfectly comprehensible to family members. Contrariwise, someone who is extruded or ostracized by his or her own system may find meaning elsewhere. Or, all within the same system, the person may be crazy at certain times or certain places only and sane at others, depending upon what the *system* is doing. Such a person may remain sane by manipulating the outer system or by changing or alternating kinship systems at different times. Again, someone may alternate, shift, manipulate, or *be* shifted out of one's system of significant others just as the system organizes coherently so that sanity is never reached.

Now let us extend our definition of psychosis, stating it in terms of systems by including all people hierarchies and by substituting "any holon" for "person" and "any adjacent holon" for "significant others." It will now read: Psychosis (craziness is a better word) occurs in a people hierarchy and is the loss of relatedness or attainment of complete autonomy of any holon vis à vis any adjacent holon. Extending the word *psychosis* in this way, we can now label families, networks, institutions, societies, or any investigatable entity as psychotic with respect to certain other entities to which it is normally related. In this model two nations may be psychotic vis-à-vis one another; an army may be psychotic with respect to its civilian superiors; or a family may be psychotic to a medical-care-delivery system,[1] but not to its own clan. Sanity then takes on a contextual meaning: Youssarian, the only sane person in Joseph Heller's novel *Catch 22* (as viewed by noncombatant readers), was obviously psychotic to his superiors, his subordinates, and his peers.

## Psychosis and Insulation

Returning to individuals and families, psychosis, according to this concept, can now be understood as the complete disengagement of a person from his or her suprasystem of signif-

[1]Again, Wynne's "rubber fence."

icant others, which is generally the family. The individual may become unrelated to any one or number of family members and thus may be psychotic with respect to some and nonpsychotic with respect to others. It will be seen, however, that in any case, once a family member becomes psychotic in relation to any other member, the family no longer is the same system.

Conversely, the disruption of a family system indicates the occurence of psychosis, so defined, between at least two parts of the system. We now can recognize that our family system definition of psychosis has become fundamentally the same as the end point of the general system process called progressive mechanization. As applied to one family member in relation to others, I call this state *insulation*.[2]

## *The Complementarity of Fusion and Insulation*

Fusion and insulation are two sides of the same coin. Just as the individuals lose their position in the hierarchy of people as their mental apparatus disorganizes, so the family becomes disconnected from the world when its inner relationships become "nonsystem." Functionally, this state is equivalent to well-known intrapsychic phenomena. That is, the merging or de-differentiating involved in some mental processes, such as sycretism and synesthesia (10) corresponds to the fusion of people within a family. On the other hand, the loosening of associations and splitting of thought and affect are part of de-

[2]To be more consistent with general system terminology, we might talk of progressive insulation (and progressive fusion). But it seems to me that to call these states (such as fusion, insulation, and even triangulation) progressive would be misleading in that doing so would imply a continuum only, whereas we are actually dealing not only with a continuum, but also with a quantum jump. A mechanism is precisely *not* a system. We suffer from this confusion because of our tendency to think *only* in time-space continuum – a prejudice that may be a function of our Indo-European language, according to Whorf (9) – and it therefore behooves us to be careful with our language. Another point which needs to be made clear is that although general system theory is most valuable as a way of thinking about organization, each system has its own local rules. For this reason I have used fusion and insulation to refer distinctly to people systems and probably, these terms should be restricted to describe process in families.

centralization within an individual and correspond on a family level, to insulation among family members.

Referring back to our basic threesome, it is self-evident that fusion of two members will insulate the third from them. Not so apparent, but equally true, is that the insulation of one member usually fuses the other two. The only other possibilities are for all three members to fuse or for all three members to insulate one from the other. In practice, this rarely happens (in my experience), presumably because, in the first instance, the mere presence of three people tends to prevent fusion, and in the second instance, the original threesome, particularly if dysfunctional, consisted of at least one member who could not stand alone. In any case, fusion of a total family would have to mean insulation from other systems; and insulation of all members for each other would mean fusion for some elsewhere.[3] Of course, fusion and insulation if sustained, mean the breakup of the family, and therefore, in family systems that actually reach these extreme conditions, fusion and insulation occur periodically and temporarily. Needless to say, such families are most unstable. Other families, although approaching fusion and insulation at times, never actually reach these points. Much more common is triangulation, discussed in the next chapter.

# Fusion and Insulation from the Clinician's View

Let us now look more closely at the clinical aspects of insulation and fusion. An individual insulated from his or her family will often display any of the common pictures of the detached or withdrawn psychotic person. Fusion on the other hand, is the loss of autonomy or attainment of total relatedness to significant others. The result is a pseudorelatedness in which

[3]For example; a runaway youngster, insulating self from family, may fuse with a religious cult.

the loss of boundaries of a person becomes such that dysfunction is as great as in psychosis.[4]

But whereas dysfunction occurs in psychosis in all those areas that demand cooperation and interdependency (communications, emotional joining, problem solving), dysfunction occurs in fusion in those enterprises that require independence and assertion of self (introspection, control of affect, innovative thinking).

Again, a wife may fuse with a husband but not with a therapist. A husband may fuse with his boss, mother-in-law, or son, but not with his wife or daughter. A common occurrence is the fusion of one member of a family with a therapist, resulting in distancing or even insulation from other members of the family. To the extent that fusion occurs among members of a family, there is insulation from other members or, in the event that all members are fused, there is insulation from the rest of the world. Thus, the finding of fusion implies the presence of insulation. Well-known examples are mother-child symbioses and *folies-à-deux*. While members of such pairs are fusing, it is impossible to engage them in a relationship; equally true is that the moment a relationship is established elsewhere, the fusion stops. It is for this reason that an outside relationship is always so threatening to a regressive twosome — Scheflen's term (11).

Both insulation and fusion are temporal processes that can be either transient (so as to result in little impairment) or sustained (so as to cause major impairment). Insulation takes one; fusion takes two, acting simultaneously. It may be easier to intervene as a therapist in the case of a fusion than with an insulated person. The odds of engaging someone are better in the fusion.

On the other hand, for a number of reasons, insulation is

[4]Extending our purview to other systems, we can see that similarly operating dysfunction can occur in satellite governments; in subsidiaries to large corporations, where administrators are undercut from the outside; in the immature marriage governed by the extended family; and so on. Note that, in each case, dysfunction occurs for both holons. Some institutions have explicit rules to prevent such occurrences, such as the army's requirements of a "chain of command" and the rule permitting the "delegation of authority but not responsibility." The need to go to a specific higher authority and the prohibition of abdication of responsibility tend to prevent insulation. The inability to bypass authority and the condonement of delegation of authority tend to prevent fusion.

more often labeled pathological than fusion is, even by family therapists. (Exceptions to this observation are probably those family therapists who have had to learn how to avoid fusion in their own original families. They can often be recognized by their tendency to remain distant.) First, regardless of our orientation, our prejudicial tendency as human beings of this era is to look at individuals, and this tendency leads to our spotting of so-called thinking disorders, a frequent attribute of the insulated person. Second, most therapists are verbal and place a positive value on talk (despite knowing that words often conceal more than they reveal), and thus the pseudorelationship of a fused couple is more often missed than is the silence or babbling of an insulated person.[5] Third, therapists, like other people, tend to be much more worried about separating people than about gluing them together; yet the labeling of a "togetherness" as pathological would require the therapist to attempt some sort of separation.

Separation is not to be taken literally here. It is a mark of our upside-down thinking that therapists do try to achieve literal separation in instances where they judge the relationship to be severely impaired, as in a mother-child symbiosis. This is precisely where neither one can tolerate separation and both need to be held together while learning to differentiate one from the other. On the other hand, in instances where people are able to function without each other, albeit with pain, and could tolerate a separation rather easily, therapists often turn themselves inside out trying to "preserve a marriage."

### *Individuality and Relatedness — Complementary Conditions of Good Functioning*

What Koestler calls the self-assertive and the integrative or self-transcendental tendencies are both present to some degree in all behavior (13). Ideally, when an individual is maturely integrated into his family, there is a balance of both tendencies, so that he "enjoys autonomy within the limits of the restraints

[5]As Zuk has noted, there is plenty of room for learning more about silence and babbling (12), and I would add that therapists often have to learn to ignore conversation.

imposed by the interests of the community. He remains an individual whole in his own right, and is even *expected* to assert his holistic character by originality, initiative, and above all, personal responsibility" (14; my italics). I would add that these expectations, verbal or nonverbal, are "performatory" in nature (15). That is, the individuals who hold these expectations are involved in a transaction with the individual toward whom they direct expectations. In the transaction, originality is elicited, including a new expectation that the other individuals will assert their originality in turn. In this way, there occurs a multiple releasing action[6] that is creative and leads to the spontaneity so highly prized in our time.

Note that both relatedness *and* autonomy are required by all involved. To the extent that one individual is expected to be unassertive, it is necessary to rely upon others for monitoring and input. To the extent that another becomes dominant in this way to satisfy the demand of others' expectations, autonomy is lost. The apparent paradox is that dominance, in the profound sense of curbing another's originality, *requires* being the originator of another's thoughts and feelings. Suppression of another with enslavement of oneself can be another description of fusion. To the extent that someone becomes assertive without regard to the community, it is necessary to ignore the expectation to present originality to the group, and therefore, that individual has no influence on the group. The self-assertion becomes a shouting in solitary; the person is insulated. A balance of joining and separateness is the *sine qua non* of the give-and-take, mutual, person-to-person relationship.

The prototype of this duality of human behavior is reflected in the finding of infantile omnipotence existing alongside the mother-child anaclitic relationship. The infant, failing to distinguish between self and others, is perceptually a whole while very much a piece of mother. Thus, every human being is born a joined individual. In adult life, both cooperative and competitive skills are required for optimum functioning and imbalances in varying degrees constitute dysfunction.

[6]Nathan W. Ackerman dubbed this phenomenon the "circular contagion."

Extreme examples of such imbalances are autism and old-fashioned back-ward schizophrenia, wherein dysfunction occurs through loss of relatedness; *folies-à-deux* and mother-child symbioses, on the other hand, reflect loss of autonomy. The former is like the excised heart beating for naught; the latter is like a vine strangling a tree until both die.

## *Fusion is a Closed, Non-viable Loop*

Consider the child who has no mind of his own, but relies wholly on mother's prompting — indeed, senses mother's mood often before she is aware herself and responds only to her. Mother, in turn, focuses every thought upon the child; worries before he can get hurt; soothes before he can get angry; reassures before he can become scared. The child, whose circuits are loaded by input from the mother, develops no skill in perceiving the rest of the world, let alone making judgments about it. Such a child is forced to use only mother's cues. As mother soothes, the child reacts with anger. As mother reassures, the child realizes there is something to be frightened about and thereby confirms mother's "knowledge" of the child. Both, then, "read each other's minds" and respond on the basis of prediction in advance of outcome, thus fulfilling the other's expectations and producing the outcome prophesized. There can, therefore, be no give and take, no unique, personal contribution to the relationship, no change and no growth. Although such a relationship has homeostatic mechanisms, it fails to "build negative entropy" because it sorely limits its input. In a word, it is a closed system. Its repertoire of interaciton is sparse and it tends to run down or blow up.

All relationships that shut out others tend to become routinized and jaded. Under these conditions, it is very difficult for a third person to influence the dyad. One must become a very special or significant other before it is possible to affect a regressive twosome and, if one succeeds, *all* one's "movements," distancing or closing vis-à-vis one of the twosome, affect the twosome and vice-versa, so that it is no longer a two-person system. Now the system has an inherent stability that allows it to be open, and further input can occur on a more casual basis; in fact, a well-lubricated threesome acts like an open system, in that it "actively tends toward a state of higher organization; that is, it may pass from a lower to a higher state of order owing to conditions in the system." In contrast, the twosome acts like a feedback system that "can 'reactively' reach a state of higher organization owing to 'learning,' i.e., information fed into the system" (16).

As von Bertalanffy observes further, "production of local conditions of higher order (and improbability) is physically possible only if 'organizational forces' of some kind enter the scene" (17).

Although von Bertalanffy is talking about the biochemical world,[7] much the same could be said for the relevance of general system theory for small groups. The "organizational forces" that I am postulating here are those derived from the twin tendencies that propel humankind toward and away from others.

## Treating Fusion

Another consequence of the organism-as-system concept is the requirement for a certain amount of "tension" and activity for optimal functioning. Without stimuli or the opportunity for activity, as in sensory-deprivation experiments, prisoner's psychosis, and retirement neurosis, the individual undergoes considerable suffering. Similarly, simple separation of fused individuals is tolerated very poorly and may result in a kind of total immobilization if another person with whom to fuse cannot be found.

A therapist may supply this need but then be unable to reasonably separate him or herself. The trick, then, is to find ways to increase autonomy so that true joining can take place. This is a painful process at best, and often, it fails. It is best done conjointly as indicted above, by bringing in a third person

[7]The quoted passage continues, "...this is the case in the formation of crystals, where 'organization forces' are represented by valences, lattice forces, etc."

to relate to both fused individuals separately, thus opening up the system and putting distance between the two fused members. The therapist may be the third party or, better yet, another member of the family may serve. In any case, the therapist strives constantly to differentiate all individuals, emphasizing each one's own responsibility for their own thoughts and feeling assessments, and demanding original responses. An inter- mediate stage in the process of going from a fusion to a three-some may be the development of triangulation (cf. Chapter V), with the potential third party serving as the semi-operative member of the triangle.

Fused individuals often cannot and will not relate directly to another person, both for (a) lack of skill and (b) the occurrence of too much anxiety. One feeds the other, because lack of intake (as in sensory deprivation) increases anxiety, and anxiety decreases learning ability. Superimposed on both may be an attitude of mistrust with regard to the "outside world" that not only increases anxiety but also promotes an active filtering out of stimuli from other than the fused system. In this sense, there is developed a skill in not relating. The task of the third party in trying to engage one or both of a fused couple is formidable, and when the natural third member (such as a distant, almost insulated father), is himself unskilled in the very tasks required, the herculean proportions of the therapy of fused twosomes can be appreciated.

## Fusion and Insulation and Psychoanalysis

In the practice of psychoanalysis, the twin tendencies to fuse and to insulate are seen in the phenomena of transference and resistance. One of the early ideas of theory of technique was to encourage the need to fuse by disengagement of the analyst and deactivation of the patient. Thus, the patient is immobilized on the couch and cannot see the therapist, and little is said to him. At exactly the same time that the patient begins to imagine or attempt getting closer to the therapist (usually in ways which are learned in the past with the original family), the need to insulate or to maintain autonomy begins to operate (utilizing previously developed skills of distancing). Distancing behavior is pointed out by the therapist and "interpreted" as being counter to the therapeutic task, while closeness-seeking behavior is simply received initially without comment (following Freud's dictum to leave the positive transference alone). There are many vicissitudes to this negotiation, but generally, since the analytic situation inherently promotes lack of contact between patient and therapist, the forces toward fusion are most prominent. When the patient becomes "aware" of the specific ways of wanting or trying to fuse with the therapist and, more importantly, the strength of the need to do so, this is "interpreted" to the patient as an infantile, unrealistic, and detrimental need. It was once thought that the patient agreed with this evaluation beause, once revealed, it is self-evident, and thereafter the patient tended to avoid such self-destructive behavior. Later, it was discovered that insight, first intellectual, then so-called emotional, was not enough, and a period of "working through" was recommended (18,19) to allow time for the patient to repeat again and again the tendency to fuse with the therapist and others in various ways, to be reminded by the therapist until he learned to remind himself to stop. Thus, in the end, psychoanalytic change of behavior patterns, like all other methods of sustained change, requires learning through practice.

Psychoanalysis, in the framework I have described, works very well (although perhaps not as quickly as other methods), despite the many difficulties of which psychoanalysts themselves are well aware (such as the tendency of the therapist to fuse with the patient, called countertransference). The trouble is that learning how not to fuse is not the end-all, be-all of health. The traditional failures of psychoanalysis, often considered people incapable of transference formation such as "severe obsessives," "narcissistic characters," and many other descriptions, are people well-skilled in distancing or already insulated. There is little room in psychoanalytic technique for the encouragement of healthy joining. The concept of the therapeutic alliance is an attempt to account for some of the cooperative facets of the psychoanalytic relationship; but it is not generally recognized that the expression of any personal feeling, including sexual feelings, may be a unique contribution to the relationship rather than a projection or displacement. Thus, attempts at healthy joining may be discouraged; indeed, it is hard to see how this may not occur unless psychoanalytic technique is broken, and such is often the case. In fact, Freud himself frequently departed from what is generally accepted as good technique, as when he gave money to the Wolf-Man (20) and other instances (21).

Nevertheless, the notion of the analyst as a "blank screen," although generally understood to be a myth, persistently influences psychoanalytic technique, so that all behavior of the patient is characteristically looked upon as emanating from the past rather than as a response to the therapist. Exceptions are when a mistake has been made or a correct interpretation has facilitated, further "unfolding of the transference." There is little opportunity to develop skill at a give-and-take relationship. On the other hand, people who need to learn healthy ways to maintain their individuality may be denied that opportunity by being labeled "resistant" when attempting to do so. It is acknowledged that such people who know too well how to fuse (such as "very dependent people") must be treated gingerly so as to avoid a "sticky transference," but little can be offered positively to increase self-assertion *within the analytic situation*; all that can be offered is the negative prevention of fusion by decreasing frequency of visits, sitting up, "reality testing," and so forth. Finally, for those who successfully learn how to stop fusing with the therapist and others, distancing maneuvers may well be learned at the expense of some ability to relate.

## Fusion and Insulation in Groups and Families

In group therapy, the twin tendencies may manifest themselves by evolvement of the group into a minicult, with derisive attacks being made upon those representatives of the outside world (usually newcomers) who defy the leader and assert their own values. The most zealous attackers are those who immediately embrace the group and subordinate what they bring from elsewhere. This phenomenon is called interface penetration by Rabkin (22). He points out that such a zealous disciple is an invader who ultimately weakens the group, but attributes this to the person being "not a stable or dependable member of the group." I would say that the more consistently such a member supported the orthodoxy of the group, the more weakening it would ultimately be. Any orthodoxy, by its nature, requires opposition to establish its "rightness." The defiant member is actually following the rules and acknowledging the importance of the orthodox point of view by defying it. The polarity between zealous disciple and defiant member constitutes a fusion, because the defiant member also requires opposition (as acknowledgement of the importance of his or her defiance). This positive feedback from disciple to rebel will eventuate in either a split, a merger, or triangulation around the leader. The defiant one is defending against a presumed loss of individuality, and the zealous disciple is avoiding insulation (and may be insulated from family of origin). In an open, nonsuppressive group, elements of both relatedness and individuality emerge in all participants. Vitality and full expression are the priorities in such a group. In the fused group, only survival counts.

In family therapy, the style of fusion most often missed is self-sacrifice masquerading as consideration for others. Many therapists tend to take on others' responsibilities as burdens themselves and may not see the unworkability of doing so. Sometimes a therapist senses something wrong with a relationship, but not having clear conceptual tools, may not be able to counter a couple's assertion that they are simply "deeply committed to each other." The refusal to relate or tendency to insulate, on the other hand, may be mistaken for a high degree of expressiveness. This is especially so among young people, for there is a disease abroad in our land called "I Gotta Be Me-itis."

## Recognizing Fusion and Insulation

When either insulation or fusion occurs in a more or less permanent fashion, it is easy to recognize. We all are familiar with both the person who does not seem to relate to another person at all and the person who is so involved in one relationship that he or she does not respond to anyone else. The transient or intermittent patterns are those that will shift with changing temporal, geographical or social contexts, and these are more difficult to discern. Insulation or the tendency to insulate by distancing, being more readily conceived from the intrapsychic point of view, is more often recognized as dysfunctional than fusion is. It is commonly acknowledged, for example, that there will be difficulty in "getting close to" people traditionally labeled obsessive or schizoid or those using the mechanism of isolation of affect. What is usually not acknowledged explicitly is that the interpersonal aspects of the person's behavior (such as a tendency to be quiet and evasive and to avoid personal interchange) are most important, if not solely important, in making such a label, whereas the intrapsychic constructions are all inferred by the labeler. For this reason, it is not generally recognized that even the original labeler might have come up with a different diagnosis if the patient had been seen in another place at a different time or with different people. Moreover, it is rarely grasped that the finding of an insulated or distancing person implies the presence of fusion elsewhere in that person's emotional system.

How does one recognize fusion? Again, it is probable that those people traditionally labeled as dependant, infantile, or lacking in ego boundaries would be prime candidates for fusion (at least with the examiner), but to me it is more fruitful to look at the interpersonal aspects directly — not only of the people fusing, but also of the distancing person. When one notes a compelling need to act in anticipation of or to prevent a direct response of a significant person to any other, one is seeing an attempt to fuse. This is not only done by parents with children as cited above, keeping another parent distant, but is also done by spouses with spouses, keeping children and grandparents distant.

When the attempt is successful (in that the significant other allows the first person to be a spokesman), this is not simply being a go-between[8] as Zuk describes(23); it is also entering into a binding two-way slavery wherein each denies responsibility and, hence, genuine outside involvement. The spokes-

[8]Other examples of go-between would come under triangulation (cf. Chapter V).

man is affirmed and supported, and speaking for oneself is avoided or, often, seen as disloyalty. "Mother knows best" or "father knows best" becomes "mother or father know everything." "I *had* to stay home or she would have been angry" is reciprocated with "John knows me so well. He can *make* me angry whenever he wants." Thus, the attribution of authorship of one's reaction or action to another is also a prime manifestation of fusion. This couple acts like a corporation that has its own policies and no principal officer to assume responsibility for them. Imagine the difficulty a child must have in trying to negotiate with such a set of parents: "We think"... "Your father always says"... "You know how your mother is." This is the "wesome" to which Murray Bowen first called my attention (24).

The reciprocity of people who fuse is demonstrated over and over by the intensification of actions calculated to start up the cycle again if one person begins to stop. For instance, in the case of a father who is "bugged" by his son's defiant antiestablishment behavior, if one can in any way influence the father to ignore his son for a time, the son, who hitherto only wanted to be left alone and "couldn't help having a bad attitude" when he was "so hassled," now will dramatically pull some bugging shenanigans never before tried. Moreover, if one can cool off the son, mother (who had been avoiding the men's fight because she "couldn't stand the conflict") may now be found to incite father by recounting son's transgressions, whereupon — having started up the hostilities again — she retires to the sidelines. Finally, it becomes clear that the fusion of two and the insulation of the third are part and parcel of the same constellation, and that one needs to open up the relationship between mother and son and between mother and father as well as to distance father and son.

## Working with the Construct of Fusion

It is clear by now that the construct of fusion is much more general and more inclusive than that of interlocking pathology or complementarity. It points to the underlying need to join rather than to the particular dynamic form that this need takes. It views the phenomena from without rather than from within, and it is from without that the therapist can be effective. In the parent-adolescent cycle of defiance and punishment cited above, one might interpret the father's projections of his own guilt for wishing to transgress, and the son's need for control due to fear of genuine assertiveness. If these interpretations and the pejorative connotations associated with them were accepted by the pair, they might well change their behavior toward one another in such a way as to change the dynamics while continuing the fusion. For instance, the adolescent might become seclusive or phobic, resulting in endless urgings to achieve or reassurances on the part of the father; or, the father may become penitent and attempt to become a permissive pal, invoking guilt in his son. Each will continue to "live in the other's head" in an endless cycle.

But if one can be taught to "stick to one's own head" and refuse to engage in the cycle (often against one's own reactions or feelings), several things happen. First, there will be a short period of relief. Second, as mentioned above, the other will attempt to stir up the old reactions all the more. Third, eventually, as the person distancing or defusing finds his feelings becoming more consistent with his actions, the other will reach out in new spontaneous ways that allow for a new order of response, to which, in turn, another response can be made. The ability to respond uniquely and openly without inhibition or distortion is the hallmark of a true relatedness. Expectations of the other person lead to inappropriate responses; they may be related to the past intrapsychically, but they are not related to the other person. History is in one's mind; a relationship is in the present.

It is to be understood that the above description of working with both or even one member of a fusion in no way diminishes the importance of the distant member of the system. It is merely one therapeutic option, and if the defusing is successful, there will automatically be more involvement of the distant member whilly-nilly. In general, it is easier and a better prognostic indication if the distant member can be included in the therapy, but this is not always possible.

It should be borne in mind that when an attempt is made to defuse a couple, either one always has the option becoming insulated. Attempting defusion is a calculated risk, requiring the exercise of fine judgment. I find family therapy to be major surgery, fraught with danger. The only salve for the therapist here is to remember that fusion is just as incapacitating and deadly as insulation.

## *Fusion as Opposed to True Relatedness*

The difference between a true relatedness and fusion may be subtle (especially since words alone can be very misleading), but unhealthy joining has two major attributes. One is the need to exclude others from the relationship, and the other is to aggrandize oneself at the expense of the other. (The second is a natural consequence of the former). It is the quality of the emotions and the intent, rather than the intensity that we are looking at here.

Underlying all is a deep-seated fear of being responsible, resulting in the abdication of authorship for one's actions and even one's feelings.

The need to exclude can be seen temporarily in any dyad at certain times, but the continual reaction to others as threats is a sure indicator that all is not well within the relationship. A man may want a woman to be complete, but a man whose identity is solely that of a woman's man is not a complete person. He is not free to be a brother, friend, nor father, let alone mentor, student, or colleague. Newlyweds wish to be alone, but if they must shut out the world to maintain the marriage, it is no marriage. In such exclusive dyads, whether they be man-woman, parent-child, or sister-brother, commonly one's meat is the other's poison. If one loses, the other wins. The theme of sacrifice and dominance is rampant. The mother has to give up her life for the child. The father feels old and inadequate as his teenaged son begins to outdo him. The wife has to worry constantly about the everyday practicalities of living and nag her dreamy and negligent husband. In such master-slave relationships, one can never tell master from slave, for the master is always a slave to the slave and the slave is always master to the master. It is an ancient law, and really the natural consequence of such arrangements, that he who surrenders himself to us is forever our responsibility (25).

In this connection, the complementarity that Toman (26) talks about, which means the matching of reciprocal relating skills in couples (as an older sister marrying one who has been a younger brother) is a double-edged sword. It is not clear from his findings, for example, whether the fact that such marriages last longer than the average means that these people function well together or are stuck together and unable to relate elsewhere. Perhaps it is fifty-fifty.

It may be evident that although the *ability* to offer and to receive makes for a healthy joining, the *need* to give or the *need* to take, particularly if reciprocal in a couple, is a good culture medium for fusion. It is important to remember that one couple can be very close and unfused, and another, not very close and fused. Fusion cannot be discriminated from healthy union by degree alone. It is the quality of joining that makes the difference. One must *be*, as well as be *with*.

# References

1. Conklin after Cowdry, Edmund, *Cancer Cells*, 2nd ed. Philadelphia: W. B. Sauders, 1955), quoted in Ludwig von Bertalanffy, *General System Theory* (New York: Braziller, 1968), 211.

2. Werner, Heinz, "The Concept of Development From a Comparative and Organismic Point of View," in Dale Harris, (ed.), *The Concept of Development* (Minneapolis: University of Minnesota Press, 1957), 126.

3. Koestler, Arthur, *The Ghost in the Machine* (New York: Macmillan, 1967), 98.

4. Wynne, Lyman C., Ryckoff, I. M., Day, J. and Hirsch, S. I., "Pseudomutuality in the Family Relations of Schizophrenics," *Psychiatry, 21* (1958), 205-220.

5. Lidz, Theodore, Fleck, Stephen and Cornelison, A., *Schizophrenia and the Family,* (New York: International Universities Press, 1966).

6. Speck, Ross V. and Attneave, Carolyn L., *Family Network* (New York: Pantheon, 1973).

7. Jones, Ernest, "The Problem of Paul Morphy: A Contribution to the Psychology of Chess" in *Essays in Applied Psychoanalysis* (London: Hogarth Press, 1951), 165-196.

8. Boszormenyi-Nagy, Ivan, "A Theory of Relationships: Experience and Transaction," in Ivan Boszormenyi-Nagy and James L. Framo, (eds.), *Intensive Family Therapy*, (New York: Harper & Row, 1965), 38-41.

9. Whorf, Benjamin L., *Language, Thought and Reality* (Cambridge: Massachusetts Institute of Technology Press, 1956), 57-64, 65-86.

10. Werner, Heinz, *Comparative Psychology of Development* (New York: International Universities Press, 1957).

11. Scheflen, Albert E., " Regressive One to One Relationships," *Psychiatric Quarterly, 34* (1960), 662-679.

12. Zuk, Gerald H., *Family Therapy: A Triadic Based Approach* ( New York: Behavioral Science Publications, 1973), 131-140.

13. Koestler, Arthur, *Ghost in the Machine,* 56-58.

14. *Ibid.,* 246-247.

15. Austin, J. L. in Rabkin, Richard, *Inner and Outer Space,* (New York: Norton, 1970), 65.

16. von Bertalanffy, Ludwig, *General System Theory* (New York: Braziller, 1968), 150.

17. *Ibid.,* 153.

18. Fenichel, Otto, *The Psychoanalytic Theory of Neuroses,* (New York: Norton, 1945), 30-31, 568-572.

19. Freud, Sigmund, "Further Recommendations on the Technique of Psychoanalysis," *Collected Papers* (London: Institute of Psychoanalysis and Hogarth Press, 1924), 23.

20. Wolf-Man, the, *The Wolf-Man* (New York: Basic Books, 1971), 113, 142.

21. Anonymous, unpublished diary of an analysand of Freud.

22. Rabkin, *Inner and Outer Space,* 149-151.

23. Zuk, *Family Therapy,* 45.

24. Bowen, Murray, personal communication.

25. Galdston, Iago, "Dynamics of the Cure in Psychiatry," *American Medical Association Archives of Neurology and Psychiatry, 70* (1953).

26. Toman, Walter, *Family Constellations* (New York: Springer, 1969), 239-240.

V
# TRIANGULATION OR THE PSEUDO-THREESOME

**t**riangulation[1] is perhaps the most prevalent and often repeated operation in all of human relations. It is a cornerstone of this book that triangulation not only avoids fusion and insulation but also is a move toward the basic threesome of human relatedness.

## The Development of Triangulation

*The Twosome is Unstable*

Imagine an ideal, mutual, give-and-take, cooperative partnership of two people. As mentioned in Chapter III, given the natural tendency to organize (progressive centralization and

[1]This process was first conceptualized by Murray Bowen (1). He says the triangle "is the basic building block of the emotional system," but sees it only as a sort of safety valve "when emotional tension in a two-person system exceeds a certain level." Moreover, he is not clear as to whether the "emotional system" is an abstract or concrete system; see Miller (2) for an excellent discussion of this confusion.

progressive segregation), this situation would not persist very long. No two people are identical, and no two people can maintain an equal distribution of power (in the sense of initiating action) for very long. Once the power distribution shifts, it tends to continue in the same direction as power begets power (sometimes owing to continuing positive feedback). For example, as one person tends to talk more, the other tends to listen. The talker becomes more adept at talking and the listener becomes more adept at listening. Moreover, the talker will develop no skill in listening and find it difficult to stop talking and the listener will develop no skill in talking and find it difficult to start talking. Often, the talker has the experience of carrying the whole load of communicating for the relationship. The listener may feel "dumped on" or demeaned. As one person gets burdened and the other becomes humiliated, resentment accumulates and the situation becomes unstable. (This would be predicted from general system theory, because increasing organization produces systems of ever higher degrees of improbability.) To allow continued interaction is painful and damaging. To decrease interaction can eventuate in the loss of the relationship (lack of any meaningful effect of one upon the other).

The most viable solution of this dilemma is the formation of a threesome that can be flexible enough to be relatively stable, yet organized enough to hold together. For many pairs, this is not acceptable. The individuals see themselves as needing the other for survival, and a full relationship with a third person is viewed as a threat. These couples do not achieve a balanced threesome, and triangulation becomes a predominant way of life.

## Pseudoresponsibility and Barricading

Husband and wife engage in conversation, trying to be together, trying to share a moment or two out of their hectic lives. They talk of the events of each other's day and soon one's statement evokes a mobilizing response in the other. The other either distances or closes.[2] Either response produces tension: Distancing evokes the possibility of loss of the relationship, and closing threatens loss of self. Perhaps the couple run out of words. Boredom sets in. He becomes absorbed in his thoughts. The wife senses his remoteness and is frightened. She moves toward him with a complaint, "You never really tell me very much." He feels smothered and protests more or less hotly, depending upon how threatened he is by his own tendency to fuse. The average couple at this point will find a third object upon which to focus. "Other men spend more time with their families." "What do you know about other men?" "You'd be surprised what I know about other men!" "What the hell do you mean by that?" And so mobility ceases and the relationship is stabilized. He doesn't get a chance to be alone with his thoughts, and she doesn't get the companionship she desires. The object can be a person treated as a nonperson or it can be an article, an idea or any group. If the object is a person, each member of the original pair can be said to be pseudoresponsible with respect to the third party. Each presumes to speak for the third. The couple can agree or disagree. The essential point is that they are riveted together emotionally on an item which occupies them simultaneously, and this prevents both distancing and closure. I call this relationship barricaded, because personal communications remain incomplete. The need for triangulation, however, implies not only a barricade that prevents ease of joining, but also a bond that mitigates against separation.

## Scapegoating

The example of triangulating most familiar to family therapists is scapegoating.[3] The trouble with this narrower concept is that it is simply what it says, namely, the placing of blame

---

[2] I am using *distance* or *close* to indicate decrease or increase of interaction. This has nothing to do with emotional climate. Hence, sitting cordially watching television is distant relative to a hot argument (closer).

[3] This term was first applied to family process and popularized by Nathan W. Ackerman (3).

upon another. If the therapist assumes that the whole operation is motivated by a need to blame, he or she is in for a few surprises. In the first place, if blaming can be reduced or eliminated, the "scapegoating" may simply take a different form, such as the need to overprotect. In the second place, a scapegoated party relieved by distancing of the couple will surely feel neglected and will try to get scapegoated again (Figure 5.1). Moreover, a distant, barricaded couple tend to insulate. Because insulation of the other two threatens the survival of the scapegoat, the scapegoat's tendency to reclaim the habitual position is reinforced. In the third place, if the scapegoat finds another or others with whom to relate, the pair will triangulate around another object. One child, for example, may then be relieved, but the basic inability of the parental couple to deal with distance and closeness will not be touched and will lead to more trouble in the future with another child (Figure 5.2).

On the other hand, if we can get one party to stop triangulating using any technique at all while maintaining the threesome, the other party will eventually stop also and deal more directly with the issues at hand. This involves training the individual to make and receive only personal, direct communications and to refuse to receive or offer communications about a third party. It is easier said than done, of course, but it does work, and it proves that the forces of the family system are more powerful than intrapsychic motivation in such instances. Scapegoating, therefore, is a much narrower concept than triangulation and is mainly of historical interest.

## Vicissitudes of Triangulation

Take a hypothetical family, for example. Mother and father argue that he is too harsh and she is too easy on their daughter. He insists on disciplining the daughter and defending the mother. She interferes and protects the daughter when the going gets rough. The daughter is not being treated as a person but is being used to hold mother and father in a fixed position. The parents can neither resolve their differences nor agree to disagree. Just as mother, by protecting daughter, disrupts any possibility of a genuine relationship between father and daughter, so father, by defending mother, forecloses the possibilities between mother and daughter.

Now if mother agrees to stay out of the problems between father and daughter and let them cope with their own differ-

Figure 5.1

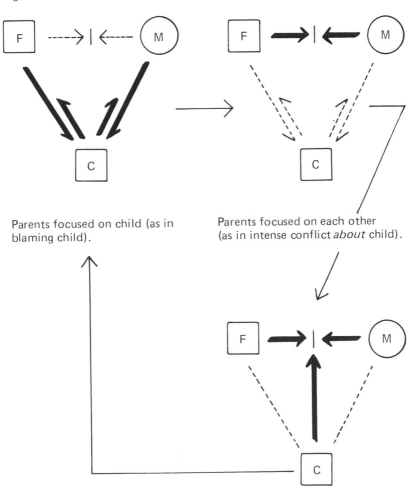

Parents focused on child (as in blaming child).

Parents focused on each other (as in intense conflict *about* child).

Child interrupts and pattern returns to original configuration.

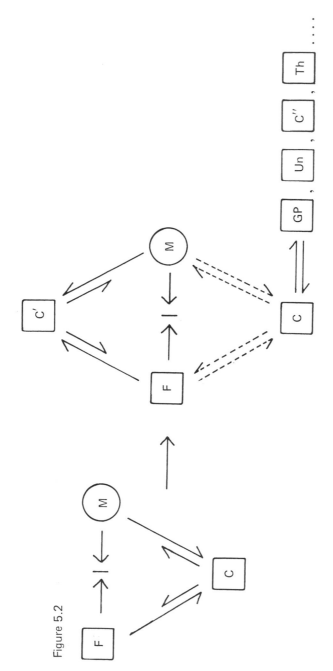

Figure 5.2

Parents focused on child.

Parents focused on second child. Grandparent, uncle, third child and therapist are potential third members of a triangle.

ences no matter what, father and daughter will face the possibility of fusing. One can be sure that not only will daughter come running to mother for support against father, but that father will also intensify his harshness, finding some brand-new techniques to get mother's goat. Yet if mother can stick to her guns and deal with daughter directly rather than get in the middle, she will find that sooner or later daughter will handle father much better than mother herself, and father will of necessity relate to daughter as a person (Figure 5.3). In order to do this, mother will have to go through a period of experiencing herself shut out and fearing for the survival of her daughter. During the course of this process, she will probably make many mistakes and tend to interfere willy-nilly. Such occasions are not only opportunities for her to appreciate the magnitude of forces acting upon her, but also can be used to demonstrate that her availability intensifies father's harshness and daughter's reactivity.

Conversely, if father can stop "defending" mother, come what may, mother and daughter will tend to fuse. Daughter will be more fresh than ever, and mother will engage in useless and frustrating, placating actions. She may even demand help from father. A steadfast refusal to play the heavy, however, will eventually result in mother learning how to toughen up when needed, and daughter will assume new responsibilities (to visualize this process simply reverse Figure 5.3). Father will have to go through much frustration with attendant outrage about his wife's degradation and daughter's impropriety. When he slips and barges in, he can note that his wife gets more overprotective or daughter gets more provocative. He will see his own contribution and how difficult it is to change. He may experience the fear underneath it all.

Simple guidance or "homework assignments," if carried out, can often generate much stronger reactions than the most blunt interpretations of scapegoating, because it is not guilt or shame that is the most intense problem to these parents, but rather the threat of fusion or insulation. Only the actual experience of distancing or closing brings this to awareness. Any meaningful action in direct relation with a significant other entails distance or closure in a sustained manner, and this

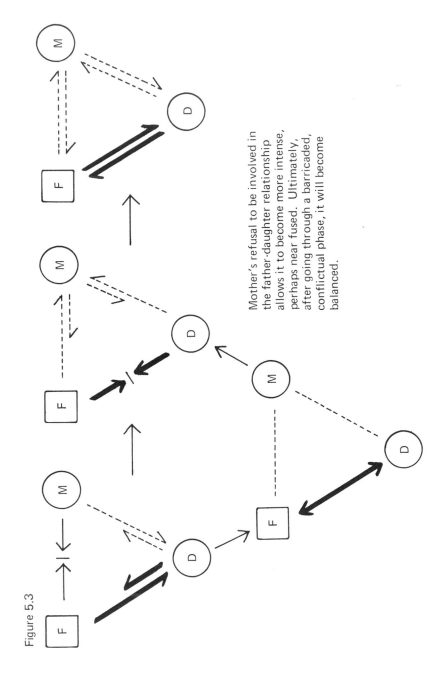

Figure 5.3

Mother's refusal to be involved in the father-daughter relationship allows it to become more intense, perhaps near fused. Ultimately, after going through a barricaded, conflictual phase, it will become balanced.

always evokes anxiety in the other. Thus, often when one mate has made an effective move toward personal freedom by refusing to triangulate, the other reports that the marriage is all finished because "I see now there is no caring." Or, as one spouse ceases to debate whose responsibility is which regarding a child, the other spouse explodes, claiming to have been trapped into becoming a slave.

Separations and blow-ups are common when bickering triangulation ceases. As stated before, however, triangulation, especially when chronic and long-term, implies a bond as well as a barrier, and these families tend not to break up. Most often, members reluctantly live with, and eventually allow and enjoy, each other's range of motion.

## Three Triangulation Patterns: A Family Typology

Knowing the triangulation pattern is a direct guide to which changes in which relationships would improve functioning. I call this the strategy of therapy. (*How* to effect the changes comprises the tactics of therapy.) If a relationship is barricaded, communications need to be completed. If a relationship is pseudoresponsible, one person needs to pay more attention to self and allow the other to initiate more of the interaction. At the same time, if a relationship is intense relative to the others, less interaction is desirable and vice-versa. Hence, the most useful typology for the therapist is a typology of process. The five general types of processes are: (a) balanced threesomes (no intervention required); (b) near-fusion (requires shifts in intensity, and triangulation may be a move toward health); (c) shifting triangles; (d) the intermediary and distant pair; (e) the entangled couple and the shut-out third. The third, fourth and fifth of these are the triangulation patterns discussed below.

*Shifting triangles* is a pattern in which the barricaded relationship moves from pair to pair in a threesome by continuous interruption of a third. (Figure 5.4) This pattern is the most frequent of all. In severely disturbed families, it occurs constantly and the family appears to be amorphous. In relatively well-functioning families, it occurs intermittently, most often in crises. It can be a reflection of the willingness of all members to assume responsibility and take leadership. Under certain circumstances, though, this can degenerate into competitive interference.

The *intermediary* is either switchboard or manager or judge for the other two, who remain distantly barricaded. (Figure 5.5) A switchboard type is nonresponsible with regard to self and overresponsive to the other two who, in turn, are pseudoresponsible toward the person playing switchboard. The manager is pseudoresponsible for the other two and neglectful of self. Often, the switchboard is a child ("tell your father to send the money" — "Mom needs the money, Dad"). The manager is often a parent ("I have to be referee in this household"), but not necessarily. The intermediary tends to be burdened and somber or resentful.

The *entangled couple* generally behave like peers in a deadlocked standoff (Figure 5.5b). Constant bickering may be the form. The bickering (or commiserating) is often focused on the third party. When communication can be made complete, the issues seem to melt away. By the same token, the attachment is not so great and splits are more frequent. The third party could be a workaholic or distant, dictatorial parent, but more likely it is a child. In the case of a child, if the pattern occurs from infancy on, the youngster can be almost inoperative in the relationship and severely impaired.

## Desired Changes or Strategies

These patterns are all processes that can only be pictured as slices of time. They can and do shift over the life of the family, particularly around the time of emerging adolescence (see Chapter VII). Moreover, they may shift from moment to moment, and various combinations occur in the same family at a given moment. This typology, therefore, is a typology of predominant patterns or patterns relevant to a presenting prob-

Figure 5.4

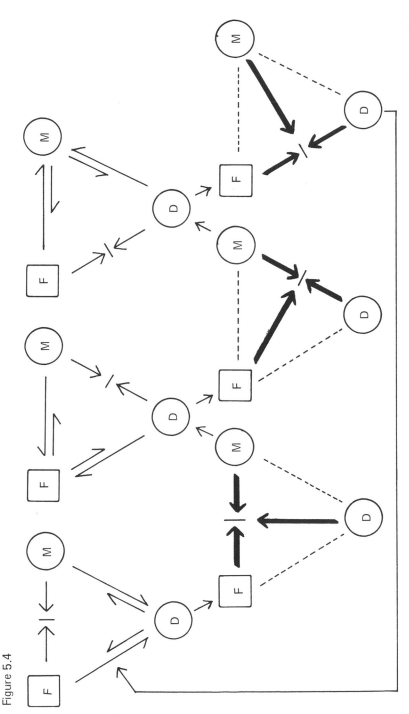

Shifting Triangles:: Each time a relationship becomes intense, the third member interrupts and begins triangulating with one of the pair. No relationship breaks up and no relationship becomes balanced.

lem. Distinguishing the pattern immediately suggests a desired change or strategy. Tactics are the means to achieve these and are idiosyncratic.

With shifting triangles, the trick is to stop the process any way one can and encourage each pair to work out their own relationship. Often, as a preliminary step, a therapist will allow members of a family to triangulate around himself (as Bowen does and Nathan Ackerman almost always did). He or she is then in a position to break up the triangulation by taking responsibility for self in relationship with any other member. Bowen usually does this by distancing or simply holding ground and refusing to engage in the triangulation process. Ackerman, on the other hand, usually would close in on one or more members with intimate and intense personal statements. Either tactic represents the same strategy of making the triangulated member more functional and opening up one relationship or making it direct so that the others tend to be renegotiated. Zuk (4) describes something similar when he discusses the therapist as a go-between (see below).

In the second type of triangulation (the intermediary), the distant pair can often be brought together by pulling out the intermediary and making each one of the pair speak for self. Note that the intermediary must also now speak for self.

Figure 5.5

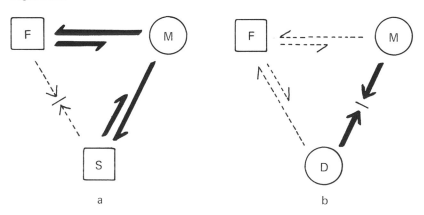

|      |      |
| ---- | ---- |
| a    | b    |
| Mother is the manager here. | Father is the shut-out third here. |

To change the third type, the entangled couple, we must either manage to make the third member heard by at least one of the other two, or we must usurp the third member altogether, using ourselves therapeutically as a significant member of the threesome who can make himself heard. This loosens up the entangled pair. An example would be the conflicted adolescent daughter and mother, who can be loosened up by getting the peripheral father to relate more to either one (Figure 5.5b). (Most therapists try to get father to interact more with the child, but getting closer to mother is just as effective.) Another example would be joining forces with the disqualified child to help him or her break up the parents' collusion.

Note that many of the above tactics make use of the principle (described in Chapter II) that total interaction in a family remains constant.

## Shifting Triangles

The example of parents focusing on a child is all too familiar to family therapists. But if one looks more closely, one often finds that the "triangulated member" can be anyone and may shift from one to another. When father is screaming at daughter to respect her mother and daughter is complaining to father about mother's intrusiveness, mother is the object and father and daughter are barricading. When daughter is crying to mother about father's violence and mother is condemning father and advising daughter to avoid him, father is the object and mother and daughter are barricading. When either of these operations gets overheated, the triangulated parent can jump in the middle as a prelude to shifting to another triangle (review Figure 5.4). In all cases, the total operation is dysfunctional. No one is talking for self in direct relation to another. There is no person-to-person relationship going.

This is not to say that triangulation is all that is occurring in this family. Indeed, when one finds that any member of a threesome can be triangulated, it implies that there is a genuine bond among the people concerned. In the above example, the father and daughter have an intense relationship of their own with legitimate conflicts, as do mother and daughter. These two relationships must be worked out in addition to the parental relationship. All three relationships, however, are explosive, and each person finds it easier to mind someone else's business than his or her own. The interesting thing about this situation is that opening up and making any one of the three relationships more direct tends to affect the other two relationships in like manner. Thus, if father and daughter begin a person-to-person relationship, there is no longer any need to triangulate around mother, mother and father can no longer triangulate around daughter (because father no longer needs to talk about daughter) and mother and daughter won't triangulate around father (because daughter no longer has the need). The other two barricaded pairs must either find someone else to triangulate about or deal with their own relationship.

Often it is not easy to see what is going on in a family. First, families tend to put up all sorts of smoke screens. Second, the picture may be complex and fluid, shifting from moment to moment. Third, and most important, our prejudices contaminate our observation and lead us astray. Persistence in thinking in terms of the individual leads us to the following state of affairs.

## *The Intermediary and the Distant Pair*
### *(Illustrating the Muddle of Inner and Outer)*

The term scapegoating illustrates the confusion in thinking about family process. From the inner or intrapsychic point of view, it means the projection of guilt or shame upon another as a defense against experiencing self-blame. From the outer or family point of view, it means the singling out of one person as the recipient of aggression, presumably to prevent more dangerous warfare between other more powerful members of the family.

Often these two operations coincide, as in the example of two parents claiming all would be well if it weren't for the bad child. Not uncommonly, though, the two processes do not coincide at all, as in the case where both parents blame each other and are overprotective toward the child. Another variation would be the constant blaming of an intimidated parent by the other while both parents actually ignore the child. In all instances, the presence of the child in the triad serves to stabilize or freeze the parental relationship, depending upon one's point of view. Parents can get neither distant nor too close while arguing about a child. In such systems, the child is a bridge but a nonperson, talked about at worst, talked at, at best. The child serves the same family function in all instances, but the individual psychodynamics are different in each, and the child cannot be said to be scapegoated from the inner point of view except in the first example. When the triangulated person is a parent, the situation can be even more confusing, because the child can indeed be scapegoated from the inner point of view, but not at all serve that function from the outer point of view. The child may even be one of the most powerful members of the family.

It is crucial that we identify which relationship is barricaded at the moment and which individual is the bridge, for the barricade implies a bond and the bridge is a sidetrack. It is the removal of the sidetrack and the enhancing of the bonds that is the end point of successful family therapy. Thus the term scapegoating, if applied *only* to picking on someone, is a useless term, whereas if it is used to connote a triangulation operation, it can be very misleading: We will have failed to be clear as to when we are talking about inner process and when we are talking about outer process.

At a showing of the videotape "A Family with a Little Fire"(5), experienced family therapists and child psychiatrists alike took for granted that the identified patient (the young daughter), at whom the mother was angry, was the scapegoat from the family point of view; viewers argued every which way about how Braulio Montalvo, the therapist, had "de-scapegoated" the daughter. All sorts of hypotheses about the mother's need to scapegoat the child were enlisted in the explanations. If one simply looked at the action, however (and listened to the narration), it was immediately apparent that the elder brother was an intermediary between mother and daughter. He tended to speak for his sister (who had started a fire), and the mother listened to what he communicated about his sister while she addressed angry comments and rhetorical questions to the girl without waiting for responses. At the same time, she was very laudatory in her remarks about the boy (who put out the fire and took responsibility for his sister), but did not address the boy about himself, nor did the boy make any statements about himself (Figure 5.6, step a). Indeed, the boy seemed to be carrying out a mission, while the mother and daughter (by her silence) seemed to bo doing their own things. Moreover, the emotional tension was obviously between mother and daughter. Thus, by the family-system definition, the boy was the scapegoat, not the girl.

The tendency of the boy to perform, rather than to be, was borne out when, shortly after the interview began, the therapist requested that he allow his sister to talk for herself and the boy tended to have little to say thereafter (although he did try several times to interpose himself between mother and daughter). Now mother and daughter had to deal with each other directly because the boy had been silenced (step b), and the therapist refused to assume the role of middleman when it was offered. (Mother tried addressing him rather than the girl.) In addition, ingenious instructions were given by the therapist to promote direct interaction between mother and daughter in and out of the session. At first there was scolding and silence, but the therapist persisted, encouraging both, and mother and daughter began to interact directly. Even in the first hour there were new developments in the relationship, and some tender affect could be noted as the tensions waned. In the second hour, after spending more time together without brother, there appeared to be further improvement. It is to be hoped that the brother, released from his intermediary function, would after a period of confusion find more autonomy (step c). To the extent that a scapegoat is one who is treated as a nonperson with a loss of self-functioning, the boy was a good candidate for the term. My preference is to discard the word entirely. Bowen might speak of the boy being "triangled in" and Zuk

Figure 5.6

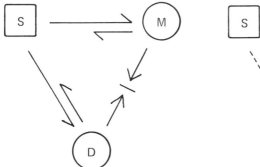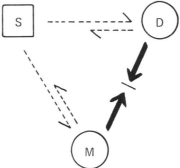

step a

Son is "parental child" and the intermediary.

step b

Distancing the son intensifies mother-daughter relationship which is barricaded.

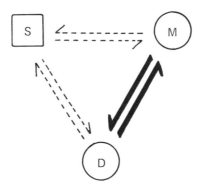

step c

Communicating breaks through barricade and results in balanced relationship.

speaks of the "go-between." I generally say "triangulated,"[4] using the nautical term for want of a better one.

In any case, the intermediary—be it a mother "protecting" the child from father, or a child carrying messages back and forth — stands in the way of the other two relating and needs to be identified before plans for his or her neutralization can be formulated and effected. This may be more difficult than it sounds, because the nuances are often subtle and the maneuvers shifting. To add to the complexity, then, by confusing what is going on inside people with what is going on between or among them, is to hopelessly muddle oneself.

### The Entangled Couple and the Shut-Out Third

This third type of triangulation most frequently takes the form of a barricaded parental pair and a shut-out third. Minuchin (6) refers to the clinical phenomena included in this process as "coalition forming." The implication is that the two coalitionists are motivated to shut out the third member and, therefore, it is easy to impute blame to the pair. Yet all experienced family therapists know from hard lessons how difficult it is to bring a distant member closer to the rest of the family even when the "coalitionists" appear to be willing to cooperate. Also, as pointed out in Chapter III, any relationship that

---

[4]I do not like the word *triangulate* either, because (as I see it) it is the threesome that degenerates into the barricaded relationship and two one-way relationships; in other words, the viable natural triangle is no longer a true triangle. The word has taken hold, however, and I haven't been able to substitute for it. The trouble with Zuk's term, which is actually a good description of one of the three way dysfunctional processes, is that he has used it to connote a power position in the family and, indeed, attributes power-drive motives to the holder of this position, once again using a term to cover both inner and outer process. He thus seems to miss the fact that the go-between is often "in the middle" and gets clobbered by both sides; that is, the go-between is often the scapegoat. Moreover, the family puts tremendous pressure on the go-between to remain the go-between. When the therapist allows himself to become the go-between, it is precisely when he subsequently refuses to continue to be just a go-between that therapeutic movement occurs. Zuk's examples of the therapist as go-between are instances of refereeing, instigating, and managing—anything but the simple courier that the term *go-between* denotes.

needs to shut out others is not mutual nor mobile; in fact, it is rigid and brittle. The need to shut out another is a way of joining through a common enemy, and the primary function is to maintain the bond rather than to exclude. This is proven by the fact that when the excluded member leaves the system (as a distant adolescent who leaves home), the barricaded pair tend to break up or else they quickly find someone else to exclude.

Here again, diagnosis is not always as easy as it sounds. The distant third may be an adolescent, for example, who passionately but only occasionally provokes mother and sullenly defies father. The parents are preoccupied with the youngster and talk incessantly about him. One may get the impression that the family is too involved with this teenager, that the parents are too intrusive and that the "boundaries are merged" between parent and child. Closer examination reveals, however, that the flareups are actually rare, that the parents hardly ever address the teenager and he never initiates interaction directly, and that, in fact, neither side is known personally to the other (Figure 5.7).

The strategy, then, becomes to increase sustained interaction between adolescent and either parent (it is ideal, but

Figure 5.7

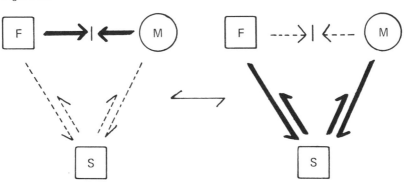

Predominant pattern

Parents intensely conflicted and ignore son.

Occasional pattern

Adolescent has provoked parents into intense intrusive behavior towards him.

generally not possible at first, for both parents to relate simultaneously to the youngster). The increased interaction actually tends to help differentiate parent from teenager and to increase the youngster's mobility outside the family, while it also loosens up the parental tendency toward intense barricading (Figure 5.8).

Assisting the parents to complete communications from one to the other would tend to accomplish the same end, but this is usually not feasible initially. Firstly, the parents object that their own relationship is not their concern, and secondly, if they attempt to forget about the adolescent, the latter usually intensifies the provocativeness and the defiance, sometimes to an extreme degree. I call this "getting in the middle."

If the entangled pair are parent and child, the shut out parent must be encouraged to interact more with either of the other two, *no matter what the form* of the interaction. If the distant parent is an ogre, so be it. The entanglement must be diminished before anything else can be accomplished.

## *Entering the System As Opposed to Engaging the System*

Sometimes it is not possible to achieve movement from the distant third, even with the alliance of the therapist. In such

Figure 5.8

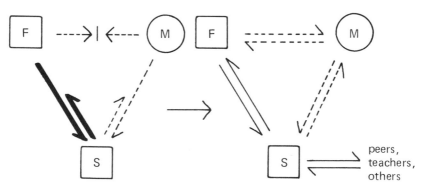

Intense sustained involvement of father and son.

Eventually leads to balanced relationships. (Father and son may go through a period of barricading and triangulating around mother first).

cases the therapist must become part of the family and make his or her own moves. In the film "The N Family" (7), Nathan W. Ackerman attempts to engage a distant, evasive family in every which way. At first, he tries to relate to any member of the family who will have him — to no avail. He tries them together, alone, and in various combinations. The moment a glance passes between parents and it looks as if they are about to interact, the eldest boy tends to jump in the middle with a diversionary topic.

Taking his cue from this oft-repeated pattern, Ackerman tries to open up the problems between boy and parents, particularly mother. Although there is obviously much potential here, the parents demure, say that the "real" problem is between themselves, and ask to be seen alone. When this request is granted, it is reported that there has been intense conflict between parents and son. They are practically mute about each other and revert to talking about the boy (see Figure 5.9, step a).

Finally, Ackerman begins to insert himself persistently and aggressively, making many "I" statements reflecting his reactions to each one of this couple individually, and challenging them to respond in kind. By the fourth session, in the wife's words, Ackerman "has become a very important figure" in their lives. There is increased interaction between them, but now they are both deeply involved with the therapist, and the son, for the moment, has been forgotten (step b). In the fifth session, they report some "loosening up" of their own relationship and some tenderness between them after many years of coldness. The wife reports an orgasm with her husband for the first time (step c). In the sixth and last session, both poignantly express their wish to continue the relationship with Ackerman. He wisely points out that they are going to have to make it in the context of their family, and particularly with the eldest boy as well as with each other, and bows out with the understanding that he may be called back as a consultant (step d).

Thus the therapist can intervene from within or without the family, depending upon personal talents and upon what is feasible for the family. By intervening from without, I mean that the therapist remains, essentially, a separate system, contiguous but not overlapping. He or she influences the family

Figure 5.9

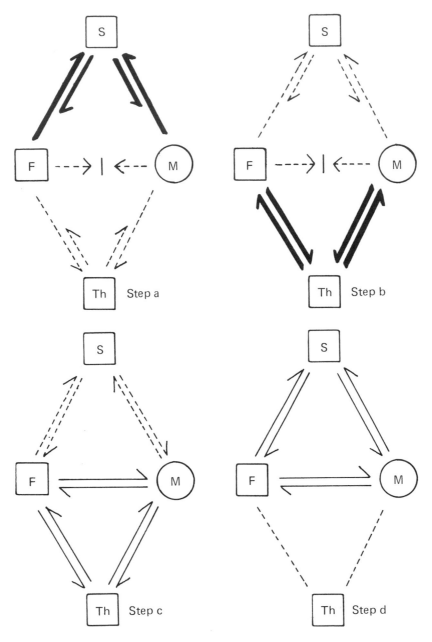

Step a: Father and mother persist in focusing on son.
Step b: Therapist forms intense, balanced relationship with each parent.
Step c: Parents break through barricade with one another.
Step d: Therapist distances and son is brought into balanced threesome.

through the prestige of an institution or the profession and the personal authority ceded by the family; by intellectual persuasion, and by a certain amount of what Carlos Castaneda called "benign trickery" (making suggestions that one knows appeal to various members, while having different motives in mind than they do). Sometimes, as in the above illustration, the therapist must become an integral part of the family system proper in order to be effectual. One becomes personally involved with the family and they with the therapist, and then one's own distancing or closing via family members exerts a profound effect. It is my conviction that this cannot be done without genuine involvement of the therapist and the willingness to expose oneself to the same forces that affect other family members. It is therefore not without a risk, and it should not be done casually. Too many people get hurt by inept overinvolvement of the therapist. If the therapist cannot be completely defenseless, allowing all emotions to operate openly, and yet maintain complete control of mobility of self vis-à-vis others in the family, the job had better be left to others. In general, it is those families whose members have the least control over their own behavior that require intervention from within.

## General Considerations

Triangulation is usually a three-member operation in which two members stabilize their relationship by focusing on a third who is treated as an object rather than a person (exceptions involving more than three people occur when one member of the triangle consists of two or more people fused into a onesome, for example, in families where twin children are treated as a single unit). To satisfy survival needs, the third member depends on the other two.[5]

In families where one individual is "the object" all the time, this person develops little skill in relating personally and often

[5]Survival needs are anything the individual needs for physical survival or anything the individual holds as necessary for survival, such as love, status, or role.

is nearly nonoperative with regard to others. He or she may be emotionally isolated or for an identity may rely totally on performance of a personal task for another, depending upon whether the other two are intensely barricaded (shutting the third out) or distant (using the third as a go-between). Other members of the family (so-called well siblings, for instance) may not be involved at all in the triangulation process so long as the major triangle continues to operate, but their investment in maintaining the status quo evidences itself quickly when an effort is made to change things. Often a favored child will support a black sheep against the parents until the parents try to ease up on the black sheep, whereupon the favored child tries to incite them against the other child again.

A family often has more than one major threesome. Of course, these are really foursomes and fivesomes, but it is easier to think of them as various combinations of threes, and the organizational forces in question truly tend to distribute themselves in this manner.

It cannot be stressed too often that we are always dealing with process, and that our static descriptions are cross-sections, mere instants in time. The longitudinal or historical point of view must be kept in mind at all time. All the operations or constellations described require intervention only if they tend to be predominant patterns, whereas all families do all these things at various times.

The most common picture in reasonably functioning families is to see the maximum number of viable threesomes operating — that is, one in a three-member family, four in a four-member family, ten in a five-member family, and so on. Frequently, any member can become the nonperson when a triangulation process is required for stabilization of the other two, and then, perhaps only moments later, return to being a separate self vis-à-vis each of the other two. It must be remembered that a father breaking up a fight between two sons is a triangulation process, as well as a child running out of the room when parents argue.

For families near fusion and insulation, triangulation is to be desired as a step toward balance. Where a nearly fused couple begin to triangulate around the therapist or another member of the family, progress is being made. A balanced threesome requires that each member, regardless of age or role, be clear about who he or she is in relation to the others, and this includes a realistic notion of their respective power or authority. That each is of equal worth and that each person's belief and affect system has its own validity in no way implies that there is identicalness or a balance of strength. Thus, the criteria of good functioning, such as maintenance of generational and sexual boundaries(8) and power and role definition(9), are included in the concept of the threesome. This derives from the fact that the threesome is defined as a system wherein each member is fully responsible for self and capable of expressing affect and belief vis-à-vis each of the other two at will.

Like fusion and insulation, the constructs of the threesome and triangulation are very high-level abstractions. Taken together, threesomes and triangulation encompass the totality of possible operations within a family system. Fusion and insulation are constructs required for the understanding of triangulation. By definition, they are only approached and do not actually occur in families; rather, they signal the demise of a family. Triangulation, on the other hand, keeps the system going.

# References

1. Bowen, Murray, "The Use of Family Theory in Clinical Practice," *Comprehensive Psychiatry*, (1966), 345-374.

2. Miller, James G., "Living Systems: Basic Concepts," in William Gray, Frederick J. Duhl, and Nicholas D. Rizzo, (eds.), *General Systems Theory and Psychiatry* (Boston: Little, Brown, 1969), 70-83.

3. Ackerman, Nathan W., *The Psychodynamics of Family Life* (New York: Basic Books, 1958).

4. Zuk, Gerald H., *Family Therapy: A Triadic-Based Approach* (New York: Behavioral Science Publications, 1971), 45-64.

5. Haley, Jay and Montalvo, Braulio, "A Family with a Little Fire," training videotape (Philadelphia Child Guidance Clinic, n.d.).

6. Minuchin, Salvador, *Families and Family Therapy* (Cambridge: Harvard University Press, 1974), 61.

7. Ackerman, Nathan W., "The N Family," unpublished film (Ackerman Family Institute, n.d.[c. 1963]).

8. Minuchin, *Families and Family Therapy*, 51-60.

9. Parsons, Talcott, "Family Structure and the Socialization of the Child," in Talcott Parsons, and Robert F. Bales, (eds.), *Family, Social and Interaction Process* (Glencoe, Ill: Free Press, 1954).

# VI
# INTER-
# GENERATIONAL
# TRANSMISSION

**a**man is brought up the black sheep of an Hungarian Jewish family. He is the rough one, the tough one. Of seven brothers, he, the second from the eldest, is the only one allowed to go into the army by his parents. The other boys' military obligations were all bought off. His parents hated one another, but agreed on his scoundrelhood (Figure 6.1). The boy, remarkable for his ability to survive, eventually ends up in a Russian prison camp, escapes, walks across Siberia, and via Hong Kong, manages to get to the United States. Here, he meets, woos, and marries a woman who is also alone and equally concerned with survival. Together, they work very hard, long hours, live frugally and save enough to open a business. Both man and woman are driving and determined, but the man is loud, gruff, and often insulting while the woman displays more finesse. Nevertheless, she is the one with the managerial disposition, and although she appears to humor her husband, she runs things her own way. His only recourse, after an impotent outburst, is to withdraw into silence, sometimes for days.

It is natural that when their son is born, the wife, now mother, takes over and the father remains distant, although sallying in an out of the emotional arena with a tirade here and there. As the son grows, he learns to obey his mother, who always gets her way, and to avoid his father, who rages irrationally. Later, he defeats his mother by innocently doing everything for her while actually ignoring her personally. He develops a dislike, almost hatred for his mother and an odd affection and admiration for his father. He remembers dimly his father's pride in him as a child and recounts his father's prodigious physical feats. As a young man, however, despite a slight awareness of his feelings, he continues to join his mother in surreptitiously deriding his father, and father remains on the outside, a thing to be feared and manipulated (Figure 6.2).

One day the young man marries. He picks a mate as unlike his mother as he can find. She wants to be lead; she wants to lean on a man. As soon as their honeymoon boat reaches the shores of Europe, he plunges enthusiastically into the role of scheduler and director. Up until then, the relationship has been idyllic. There is nothing but togetherness. Now there are activities on activities, and the woman soon realizes that she

Figure 6.1

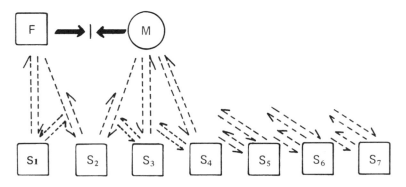

Parents single out the second son and take a pseudoresponsible attitude towards him while maintaining balanced but distant relationships with others.

is more alone than ever. Her husband is leading her into the busiest of schedules, which he fancies is her heart's desire, but he does not stop to consult her, nor does she speak up. He is forever looking for positive responses from her, as he assumes she loves activity as he does. She wants some quiet. Ultimately, she feels ignored and resentful, and he feels misunderstood and confused. They do not communicate. The situation is fast becoming explosive when the day is saved by pregnancy and the birth of a girl. Now they have something else to focus on (Figure 6.3).

Figure 6.2

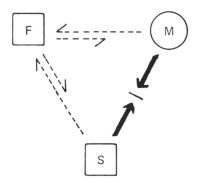

Mother and son commiserate about and ally against father.

Figure 6.3

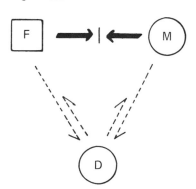

Mother and father do not communicate about each other. Their relationship is about their daughter.

In this instance, the parents are both awed by the child. They are frightened and feel inadequate, and they worry together. They get little or no help from their extended families, but there is some comfort in both being in the same boat. Their personal difficulties with one another are forgotten. As the child grows, she learns that she can get what she wants from her parents by worrying them. She can actually intimidate them. She becomes tough and demanding, oftentimes raising hell when things don't go her way. Yet she remains distant and misses out on the warmth and tenderness her parents could have given to her. The circle is complete. The girl is her own grandfather. Her father holds the same position as *his* grandfather (Figure 6.4). Diagrammatically, each successive generation is a mirror-image of its forbears.

Figure 6.4

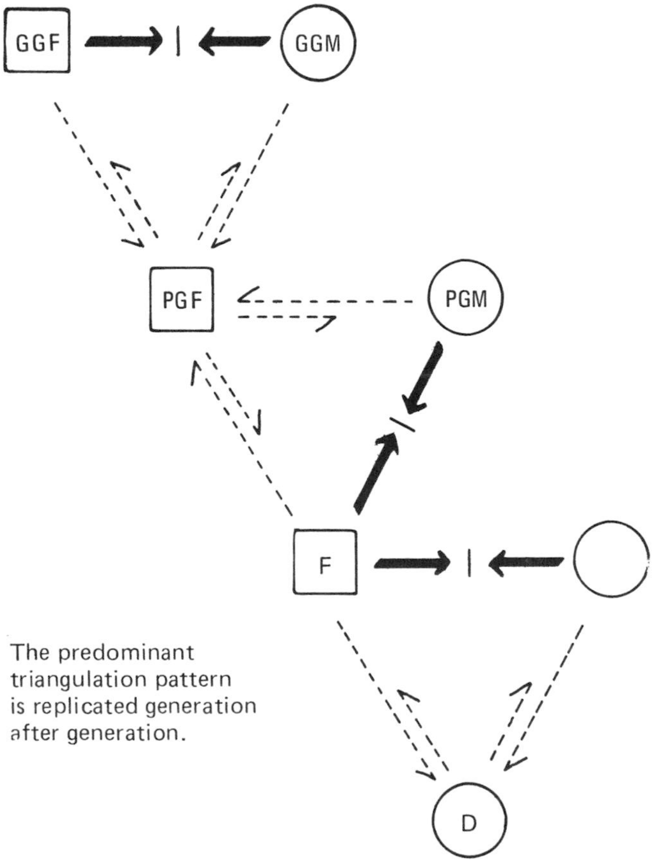

The predominant triangulation pattern is replicated generation after generation.

# The Replication of Family Constellations

What is being transmitted here is not a personality but, rather, the actual family constellation from generation to generation. The skip-generation phenomenon with which we are familiar (such as alcoholics who give rise to teetotalers who, in turn, raise alcoholics) is an adventitious result of the replication of the major family triangulation patterns of threesomes. I use the term constellation to signify the specific intensity and type of these relationships. Intensity is the amount of interaction. Type refers to whether a relationship is balanced, pseudoresponsible, barricaded, tending to fuse, or tending to insulate (see Chapter V).

Note that replication of the family constellation does not mean that parents do the same with their children as was done with them. On the contrary, people tend to do the same thing with their children as they did with their parents, and it is this fact that gives rise to the skip-generation phenomenon. When we think in threes instead of twos and see that people do with their spouses and, simultaneously, their children the same thing that they did with their parents, we see that the skip-generation phenomenon is nothing but a partial instance of the larger principle of intergenerational transmission of family constellation. I hold that this principle is a general tendency for all human families and that it occurs with remarkable regularity, despite the many apparent intrusions of life. Often, the family constellations of two extended families match in such a way as to provide a replication of both extended families in the new family. In the above illustration, the maternal grandmother of our young girl was often preoccupied and noncommunicative. *Her* daughter (our mother) had to take charge and yet maintain a semblance of submission. The maternal grandfather was an imperious ne'er-do-well who lived off others and would appear on the family scene for an exploitive period, only to disappear when he had gotten what he could until the next time. Our mother was the big sister who alternated with her mother in trying to get father to assume responsibility (Figure 6.5). Thus, both parents had a barricaded relationship with the respective grandmother and a pseudoresponsible one with grandfather. The little girl held the position of both grandfathers, while the spouses held the position of each other's respective mothers (Figure 6.6). This is not to say that they necessarily resembled the parent of the other, but that the general nature of the relationship was similar.

### *The Individual Can be Molded to Fit the Family*

A more remarkable phenomenon occurs when the two extended families do not jibe. In this case, one of the families is dominant, and the spouse from the other family alters his or her general mode of operation to fit. Here we see true adaptability, and we are reminded that life is the best therapist; that is to say, individual psychodynamics sometimes change more readily during the natural course of events than in therapy. There is nothing magical in this. Everyone's character has at least two sides, and in many people, there are several. Thus, in the above-cited history, the second-generation wife had broken away from her mother before she met her husband and had developed another side of herself. She lived alone and had a strong social network within which, to her own surprise, she was able to function in a self-assertive manner. This was a side

Figure 6.5

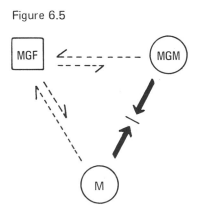

Grandmother and mother's relationship revolves about grandfather's non-responsibility.

that had developed earlier during her mother's hospitalization. When she married, under the influence of her husband and his original family, she reverted to her earlier mode of behavior. Years later, when the growing of her child into a woman forced the family into therapy, the wife again became assertive and dominant, while the husband lost his ebullient self and became subdued and clinging (Figure 6.7). This was an old side of him vis-à-vis his dominant mother before he learned how to defeat her. Note what occurred was a near-fusion.

### Intense Involvement with a Spouse's Family of Origin Is Not Unusual

Still another aspect of this complicated process is that a spouse may get caught up in the triangulations of the other spouse's family. Again, in our example, the wife became a

Figure 6.6

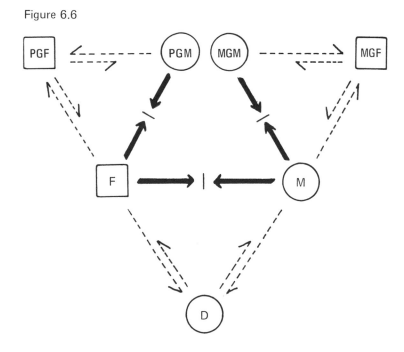

Paternal and maternal original family constellations are mirror images of the present family constellation.

significant other to the paternal grandmother and grandfather. She could not tolerate the grandmother's controlling ways, yet overt animosity never flared between the two women. Rather, any flareups were between wife and father-in-law, who in turn withdrew, and then it was the wife's job to pursue him and coax him back, much as she sometimes did as a youngster with her own father. Everyone sympathized with her; but her own self and the issues she needed to open up between herself and her spouse and between herself and her mother-in-law got lost in the shuffle (Figure 6.8). Note that her husband became more distant from his parents and that *their* difficulties were swept under the rug.

## *Intergenerational Transmission Theory Can Illuminate the Behavior of an Individual*

The principle I am expounding here can often give us a picture of the forces acting on an individual and the powerful implications thereof. A good example is the following family history. A young man is deserted by his father at the age of

Figure 6.7

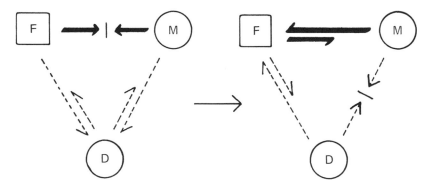

Early marriage replicates early pattern of mother.

Later marriage replicates pattern mother developed as young woman. Note that all that changes in mother's repertoire is the intensity.

sixteen. He says, "My father left me without carfare and I would never do that to anyone." His father, a distant person, had been pursued by mother and son throughout the family life until the father's abandonment. The relationship between mother and son is described as cordial, superficial and not personal (Figure 6.9). The young man is industrious, does well on his own, and marries a woman who seems to be a good match and with whom he has a "nice" if passionless relationship. She had been used to catering to her mother, who made demands with silence. With her father, she had maintained a friendly, distant relationship (Figure 6.10).

This woman testifies that in the beginning of her marriage, she used to try to cater to her husband but soon gave up when she realized that he fled her ministrations. Fortunately, a son is born very soon, and the woman, now mother, is able to "put her all" into the boy, living for his whim. The new father becomes intensely interested in the boy and, being a traveling man, alternately is extremely involved and absent. In time, this evolves into a two-way pattern, as the boy finds his father's constant advice, lectures, and intermittent foisting of presents upon him unbearable and rebuffs the father if father does not

Figure 6.8

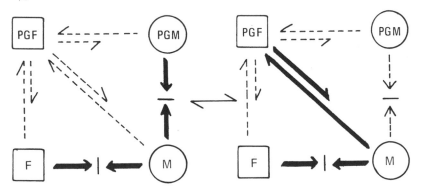

Paternal grandfather withdraws and relationship between mother and paternal grandmother is intensely barricaded.

Mother woos paternal grandfather back and tension between the two women eases.

leave beforehand. This interaction turns out to be remarkably similar to that between father and grandfather (Figure 6.11).

The boy becomes a self-indulgent ne'er-do-well young man, and, when father tries to change his ways, mother supplies the young man with funds behind father's back. Actually, the father knows but figures he cannot do anything about it without jeopardizing the entente between him and his wife. Now the young man marries a nurse who appears cold and distant, not suffocating like his mother. She turns out to relate to him, in fact, more like his father, berating him periodically for his behavior and then withdrawing. To complete the picture, they

Figure 6.9

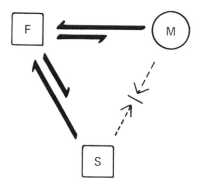

Mother and son cater to and place demands on father.

Figure 6.10

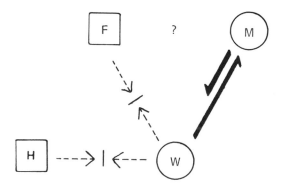

Wife remains attached to her mother and is in a cordial, barricaded relationship with father and husband.

have a son, who, from a very early age, pursues the young father and maintains a distant, utilitarian relationship with the mother just as his grandfather did before him. When one looks at all the forces impinging upon this young man wonders how he stays put. He doesn't. He deserts the scene like his grandfather by becoming a heroin addict.[1]

## Beyond Threesomes

In the above two examples, I demonstrate the power of observing in threes rather than in twos. For the purpose of illustration, however, I have deliberately simplified the situa-

Figure 6.11

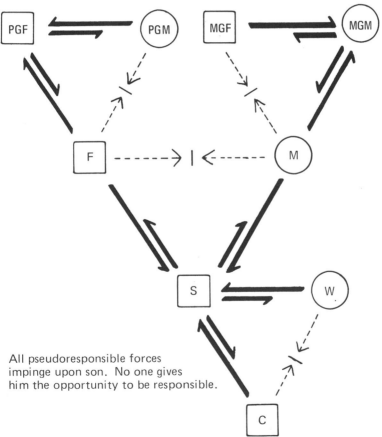

All pseudoresponsible forces impinge upon son. No one gives him the opportunity to be responsible.

[1]The constellation depicted in Figure 6.11 is typical of a substance-abusing family.

tion, as I often do in my own clinical work. (As indicated in
Chapter V, it is expedient to use building blocks of threes in
looking at a family, rather than to try to envision the totality
of emotional fields acting at any given moment.) We must bear
in mind, then, that everyone can and does participate in more
than one threesome and, moreover, will behave differently in
different threesomes within the same family. In our first example, a second girl was born to the young couple. In relation
to this daughter (see Figure 6.12), the mother tended to be her
pseudoresponsible self (behaving as she had with her siblings),
while the father tended to be distant (behaving as he had with
his sibling). Note that again the spouses relate to one another
as they did to their respective mothers, but the specific content
of the relationship is different in this threesome than it was in
the threesome that included the father. Both parents were
intimidated by and commiserated with each other over the first
child. The second child was jealously protected by the mother,
and the father mostly withdrew. Occasionally, he fought with

Figure 6.12

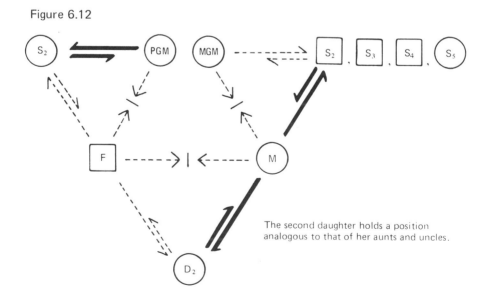

The second daughter holds a position
analogous to that of her aunts and uncles.

mother over his exclusion (rather than establish an actual relationship of his own with the girl).

In the second example, there were also siblings. These were ignored by the parents as compared to the first son and they tended to get in the middle of the parents' relationship as disrupters. They were fraternal twins who often would have terrible fights or trouble in school whenever the parents' relationship became more intense (Figure 6.13). Again, the parents' relationship remained the same, yet each parent was different

Figure 6.13

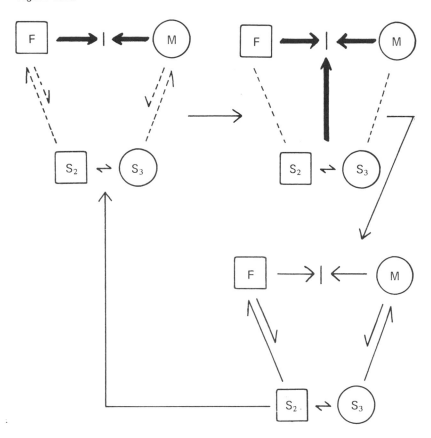

When the parental relationship becomes intense, the twins disrupt. The parents react, intensifying the parent-twins relationship and deintensifying the parental relationship.

with each sibling: The parents related to each other as each did to his or her own parent of the opposite sex; but when the first-born was distancing, they tended to join forces, whereas when the twins remained distant, the parents remained distant for the most part. Whenever they increased their interaction, the twins tended to disrupt, whereupon the parents distanced from one another by triangulating around the twins, and the twins again distanced.

As one studies more, one sees that there was a reciprocal relationship to the movements of the siblings; namely, it was after the first-born sibling would pull away and the parents converged that the twins would break it up. The first-born would then return to mother (for money, for instance), and the twins would ease off until the next time. This remarkable ebb and flow can often be seen across the generations, keeping the family in balance. In this example, when the eldest son distanced, the mother would move toward her own mother, who sent out demand signals just in time (Figure 6.14). This process, in coordination with the twins, also prevented too much closeness between husband and wife (Figure 6.15).

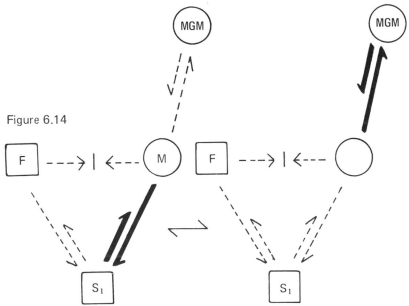

Figure 6.14

The intensities of the mother-oldest son relationship and the mother-grandmother relationship are inversely proportional.

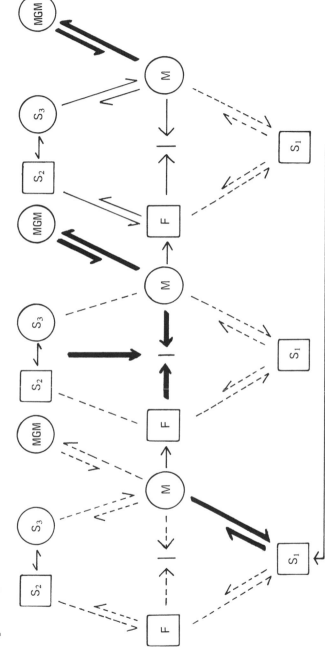

Figure 6.15

Shifts in intensity are coordinated. The mother-son relationship alternates with the mother-father relationship and the mother-maternal grandmother relationship. The marriage, in turn, is monitored by the twins (sibling two and three) whose involvement will deintensify the marriage.

In sum, then, the family clan is a complex of interlocking relationships, the pattern of which tends to replicate itself as a mirror image from generation to generation. The rule of constancy of amount of interaction originally given for nuclear families, also holds for clans, so that increase in interaction within one generation decreases it within another and vice-versa. One can use this effect to therapeutic advantage, as will be seen in Chapter VII. The illuminating power of this theory will also become more evident.

CHAPTER **VII**
# THE FAMILY
# WITH
# ADOLESCENTS

**l**ess than two decades ago, family therapists such as Nathan
W. Ackerman (1) and John Elderken Bell (2) were pleading
with the psychotherapeutic community to look closely at the
family in connection with the assessment of adolescent problems. Now, almost casually and without any fanfare, we take
the quantum leap of giving primacy to the social unit of interaction, in this case the family, and ask, What effects do individuals and events have upon it? It may be that the dramatic
shift has not been noticed because our central interest, the
human being, has not changed. It is simply that we finally see
that man is not a solitary traveler moving through an environ-

This chapter first appeared in Elizabeth Carter and Monica McGoldrick (eds.),
*The Family Life Cycle* (New York: Gardner Press, 1980). It is reprinted here
because it contains many clinical examples that illustrate the principles described in Chapters I through VI. It also contains a summary of the theory, which
will serve as a good review if the reader accepts the redundancy. I have made
several minor changes in this version.

ment; he is part of the environment and, perhaps, an "indispensable element of nature" at that, exhibiting "the fragility and vulnerability that always accompany high specialization in biology" (3). Looking at the family, the cradle and emotional headquarters of humanity, may therefore be part and parcel of some dull apperception of ours that the human race is an endangered species.

And no one can "hoist danger signals" more loudly and dramatically than adolescents (1). On the international scene, storms of adolescent protest are surefire indicators that governments or societies are sleeping or headed into blind alleys. On the family level, it means, "Mom and Dad better get it together before I go out on my own for good." This is one end of the spectrum of ordinary development wherein a family muddles along, functioning passably with unresolved parental or extended family problems at the expense of one or more individual's growth. At the other end, well-lubricated family organizations can enjoy the antics of the adolescent and enrich themselves with the torrent of information that is theirs for the listening. The adolescent challenges the family daily with new styles, new language, new mannerisms, new values for behavior and news of the world, especially the world of youth. More than any other family member, the adolescent is not only a conduit to the world at large, but also a bridge between old and new. Functioning as "his majesty's loyal opposition," the teenager can be harshly critical and brutally frank, but rarely dull. At times, in the midst of pushing an adult to the wall with various provocations or testing of authority, a sudden exposure of vulnerability or total childlike trust and affection can melt the heart. It is just this mix of child and adult that confuses the family in its dealings with the adolescent member. Should this pronouncement or that bit of behavior be taken very seriously or just passed over lightly? Is this new interest or activity a passing fancy or a new trend that needs to be nipped in the bud or incorporated into family life? Is this friend or that group just a chance meeting or must the relationship be evaluated for its possible impact on the family? Is it possible to assess all the teenager brings home? Is there time? How much can the family pry? When to set limits? When to let grow?

Truly it is impossible to raise teenagers. In the end they

must use what they have and meet the world on their own as best they can. If the family can roll with the punches and learn something of the latest generation from their teen, they will remain a haven for the return of the adolescent from time to time when toes are stubbed and knees are bruised. In the long term, if the family can take care of itself, it will be doing the best thing for the adolescent. The saving grace is that with all the turbulence and instability characteristic of adolescent growth, the ordinary teenager retains a playfulness and sense of humor that is easily tapped. And the spurt of growth with its release of new yet ancient biological rhythms is exciting and potentially rewarding for those who will partake of it.

## Family Organization

The ideal family is organized around balanced threesomes (see Figure 7.1), as I have described in Chapter III. Each relationship is a mutual give and take, each person taking responsibility for self *according to his or her natural capability* and neither overfunctioning nor underfunctioning. Note that this definition can be applied to infants or the handicapped and certainly to adolescents. The transactions of each relationship are open to all other relationships in the family and therefore affect, and are affected by, all other relationships. Moreover, the intensity of each relationship, measured by the rate of interaction, is the same ($a = b = c$) over a reasonable period of time.[1] This means that no one is shut out and no one is swallowed up. At the same time, each relationship is mobile; that is, each individual is free to increase interaction ("let's make love" or "I have a bone to pick with you") or decrease interaction ("I want to be quiet" or "I'm interested in something else now") at any given moment. Finally, there is a free flow of communications outside the family; any member is free to relate to nonmembers and does so.

In any balanced threesome, the toal amount of interaction

[1]Clearly, a large increase or decrease in interaction between any two members over a one-day period does not indicate an imbalance, whereas a lesser change among people living together over several weeks must be significant.

remains approximately the same $(a + b + c \approx k)$. This means that if one relationship becomes more intense, another one, or generally two, become less intense. Conversely, if one member of a threesome withdraws, the other two are drawn together (Figure 7.2). It is an apparent paradox that a stable family is one that is most fluid. To tolerate new arrivals, death, or illness, all relationships must be flexible. (The diagram becomes much more complex when other members are added; for example, our old-fashioned family of six has fifteen relationships and twenty threesomes, but the principles are the same.)

One must also consider the reciprocal effects of extended family and nuclear family. An individual generally relates to members of his or her nuclear family in the same manner as he or she learned to relate to the original family. An overfunc-

Figure 7.1

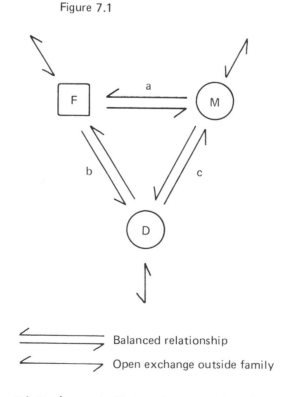

Balanced relationship

Open exchange outside family

$a \cong b \cong c$ (amount of interaction approximately equal)

tioning parent, for example, is often simply repeating the early experience of having grown up with an underfunctioning parent. The parent may rationalize this behavior by saying that it is a deliberate attempt not to make the same mistakes as the grandparent, to spare the third generation the pain of the second, and to "prevent my children from having the same hangups as me." The result is that the third generation turns out to

Figure 7.2

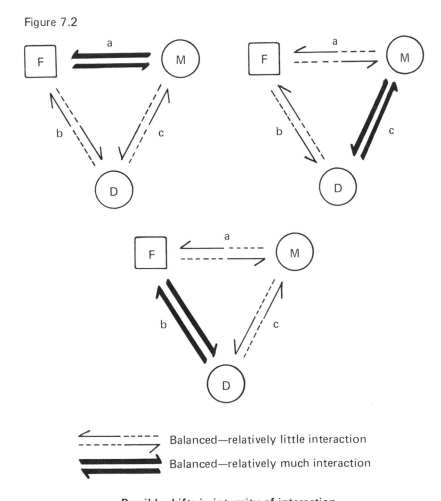

Balanced—relatively little interaction

Balanced—relatively much interaction

**Possible shifts in intensity of interaction**

$a + b + c \cong k$  (sum of all interactions approximately constant)

be like the first. The child of an underfunctioning parent rears
an underfunctioning child. A mother, used to an intense relationship with her mother and little interaction with her father,
may repeat this pattern with her daughter and husband. Moreover, the relationship between daughter and husband will tend
to mimic the relationship between the grandparents in both
quality and intensity. It is amazing how often the relationships
in the nuclear family tend to be mirror images of both extended
families. This means that the child, particularly the adolescent,
may often become a special kind of peer of a grandparent,
either competing for nurturing or control, or participating in a
sympathetic alliance. The rules of intensity also apply here.
When the adolescent either makes demands on the parent
(increasing intensity) or rejects the parent (decreasing intensity), there tends to be a reciprocal decrease or increase in the
parent-grandparent relationship. This, in turn, affects the
grandparents' marriage. Conversely, retirement, illness, migra-
tion and, of course, death of a grandparent often have profound
consequences for the parent-child relationship and the parents'
marriage.

Therefore, of all the natural events that occur in the family
life cycle, the emergence of adolescence is the one most likely
to test the flexibility of the family organization. This is not due
to the dramatic changes adolescents can exhibit in relation to
other members of the family, nor is it simply because adolescents can move from one extreme to another in a trice allowing
little time for adaptation. It is because the adolescent moves
rapidly and with wide range in all three major parameters of
family organization that the health of the family may be sorely
threatened.

## The Adolescent and Responsibility

The adolescent overfunctions one minute and underfunc-
tions the next. He or she wants total responsibility for self or
none at all; indeed, being a "tweenager" may be inherently
incompatible with balance of responsibility, and the clinician
is hard put to evaluate the health of an adolescent relationship
in these terms. (It is fascinating to speculate here that a major

function of so-called adolescent instability is to prevent fusion; that is, entrenchment of the underfunctioning or over functioning side vis-à-vis a significant other.) In turn, each and every member of the family must bend if a working relationship is to be maintained with the adolescent. Big brothers must be able to become peers at times and even little brothers. Little sisters may suddenly find themselves confidantes. Parents may have to coddle at times and allow themselves to be looked after tenderly at others. Grandparents, after whom the teenager is modeled by his or her parents, may find themselves the target of sudden hostility or surprising endearments. Everyone's mettle is tested. Everyone has a chance to grow.

## The Adolescent and Intensity

At the same time, the adolescent is rapidly changing the intensities of his or her relationships. The young girl who used to cuddle with her daddy, now becoming a woman and sensing her father's awkwardness, rebuffs him shyly. Father, somewhat confused and angry, may maintain contact by means of an endless cycle of condemnation against her rebellion, or may turn to mother with demands for which she is unprepared. Daughter, too, may now turn to mother for more nurturing or control. The beleaguered mother is now pulled away from her mother, whom she has been parenting (Figure 7.3). The ramifications are deep and the ripple effect is wide. I have seen grandparents' marriages of forty years suddenly become intolerable under such circumstances. A young man, intensely engrossed in his own pursuits for the time being, may so force the parents to look at each other that they must deal for the first time with such issues as lack of companionship, sexual difficulties, or dominance. The results can be explosive (Figure 7.4).

## The Adolescent and Extrafamilial Relationships

Finally, the adolescent is a peer-grouper and explorer *par excellence,* forever sallying forth into the community and

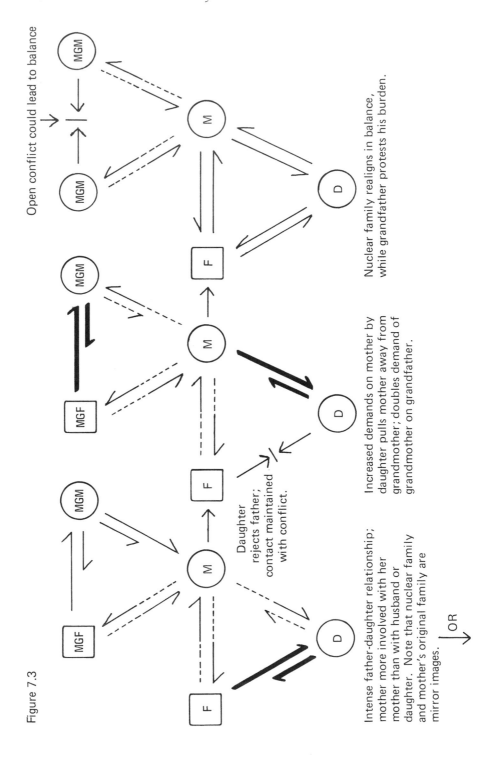

Figure 7.3

Open conflict could lead to balance

Daughter rejects father; contact maintained with conflict.

Intense father-daughter relationship; mother more involved with her mother than with husband or daughter. Note that nuclear family and mother's original family are mirror images.

Increased demands on mother by daughter pulls mother away from grandmother; doubles demand of grandmother on grandfather.

Nuclear family realigns in balance, while grandfather protests his burden.

OR

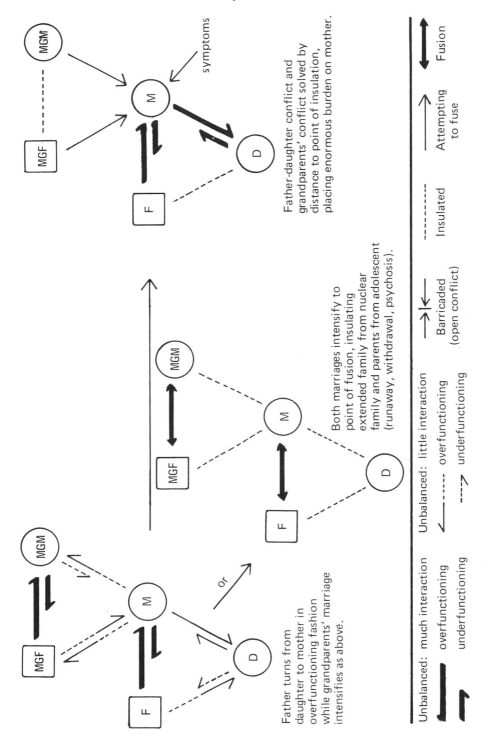

symptoms

Father-daughter conflict and grandparents' conflict solved by distance to point of insulation, placing enormous burden on mother.

Both marriages intensify to point of fusion, insulating extended family from nuclear family and parents from adolescent (runaway, withdrawal, psychosis).

Father turns from daughter to mother in overfunctioning fashion while grandparents' marriage intensifies as above.

or

Unbalanced: much interaction
overfunctioning
underfunctioning

Unbalanced: little interaction
overfunctioning
underfunctioning

Barricaded (open conflict)

Insulated

Attempting to fuse

Fusion

Figure 7.4

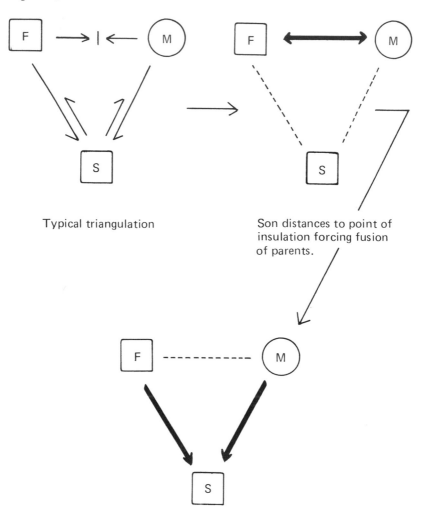

Typical triangulation

Son distances to point of insulation forcing fusion of parents.

Marriage explodes (e.g., divorce). Each parent pursues son.

bringing back new ideas, experimenting with new modes of behavior, and offering new values. More than that, he or she is forever bringing in new people (literally or figuratively, depending how receptive the family is), many of whom are more or less alien. This is always somewhat of a threat to the family. In the first place, it forecasts the eventual leaving of the individual, the natural demise of the family and the involution of the parents. This is an ordinary event that occurs to all, but it can be looked upon with equanimity by only a few. Secondly, the new input forces the family to reevaluate itself, often painfully. The adolescent frequently becomes a critic, exposes hypocrisies, and undermines long-standing prejudices. A young man, finding himself newly interested in the arts, defies his father and refuses to go into the family business and compete for materialistic things to make up for his father's lack of success. The father must now face his own sense of failure and perhaps look at *his* father's overcompetitiveness with him as, meanwhile, grandfather berates him for not controlling son (Figure 7.5). Or a young woman, demanding that she be given a chance to carve out a career, eschews marriage and children while pointing to the unfulfilled drudgery of the mother and the emptiness of the parental relationship. The mother, in turn, may be stirred to remember the pooh-poohing of her childhood ambition to be a nurse and even take it up with *her* father (Figure 7.6). Again, the effects of adolescent happenings may be far-reaching and soul-shaking.

To repeat, three major aspects of family organization are regularly and simultaneously being shifted in families with ordinary adolescents. The balance of responsibility along the overfunctioning-underfunctioning axis in each relationship seesaws. There are marked shifts in intensity of interaction of some relationships with concomitant compensations in others. There is a great surge of exchange with the community at large, with input coming not only from the adolescent and friends, but also from teachers, other parents, and officials, while the family must necessarily expose itself through the same process.

Figure 7.5

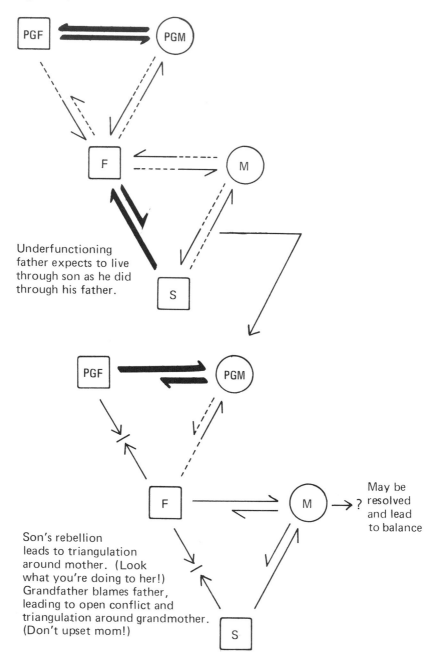

Underfunctioning
father expects to live
through son as he did
through his father.

Son's rebellion
leads to triangulation
around mother. (Look
what you're doing to her!)
Grandfather blames father,
leading to open conflict and
triangulation around grandmother.
(Don't upset mom!)

May be
? resolved
and lead
to balance

# Treatment of the Family with Adolescents

It is no wonder, then, that so many families come to treatment with adolescents. Or maybe these families are simply more memorable — eight out of eleven well-known family therapists chose families with adolescents for their detailed presentations in Papp's anthology of family therapy case studies (4). As noted before, the average family seems to weather the storm, adapt to it and grow. I only know this from retrospective studies done with families who reared adolescents and escaped therapy, but then came to family therapy later for other reasons. It has been my observation that all these families realigned in some way and renegotiated relationships for the better. Others come apart at the seams. I haven't seen families

Figure 7.6

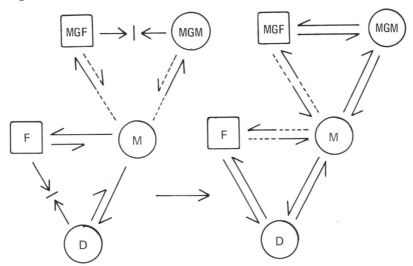

Overfunctioning mother expects daughter to be the "good wife" as she was the "good daughter" to her father.

Note that original barricading of grandparents' marriage is replicated in father-daughter relationship.

Assertion of daughter as adult with both parents leads to assertion of mother with her father and husband, concomitant with or preceded by alliance of maternal grandmother and granddaughter. All relationships become renegotiated and balanced.

simply muddle through, maintaining old patterns as they may
in the case of other major events like birth and death. This
finding again speaks for adolescence being a very special nodal
point in family life.

It is well known that adolescence is a common time for the
onset of major mental illness. This is apparently associated
with the biologic fragility of the adolescent combined with the
almost inevitable decreased involvement of adolescent with
family. The adolescent may leave home or become deeply
involved in outside affairs. The family may be unable to partake of adolescent happenings or comprehend adolescent
ways. The loss of emotional headquarters can lead to breakdown. Once breakdown actually occurs, however, the family
is dealing with many factors above and beyond those peculiar
to adolescence. Catastrophic illness, acute or chronic, generally
means involvement with outside authorities and the whole
mental health care delivery apparatus. At this point, a family
therapist, even in a hospital setting, frequently has little control
over the situation. The most important thing one can do then
is to help the family maintain contact with the adolescent in
as meaningful a way as possible while focusing on other relationships that need help.

I should like to offer now some remarks regarding some
families who present themselves for help with adolescents,
paying particular attention to the effect the adolescent has had
on the family.

The four possible ways that families with adolescents may
present themselves are the same as any other family, namely,
(a) symptomatic behavior of the adolescent (frequently a
school referral); (b) trouble in the marriage; (c) symptomatic
behavior of a sibling (usually a younger sibling who is noticed
or picked on more intensely since the adolescent has distanced
or refused to be triangulated); and (d) sypmtomatic behavior
of one of the parents (frequently with extended-family problems). Regardless of the manner of presentation, all four of the
above phenomena are involved to some degree; and all three
of the process parameters already described are always present
(responsiblity, intensity and extrafamilial interaction). For
clinical purposes, the manner of presentation is relatively un-

important except that one must always bear in mind that only the tip of the iceberg is offered. A marital problem is always much more than just that. Our evaluation of process, which is tantamount to family diagnosis, is much more important, for the predominant patterns discernable provide the best clues for effective intervention.

## Symptomatic Behavior of the Adolescent

Symptomatic behavior of the adolescent is a commonplace. The adolescent is either increasing or decreasing intensity of involvement with family. Examples of the former are intense involvement with peers, general withdrawal into self, and "rebellious" running away. Examples of the latter are shifting from one parent to another and speaking for self vis-à-vis both parents who had been triangulating about the adolescent. The latter is also frequently labeled rebellion. In the first instance, the therapist must help the parents to keep in contact with the adolescent without chasing after him or her. They must be available and responsive when the adolescent moves toward them. Often this involves overcoming their own feelings of rejection and recognizing even hostile responses of the adolescent as signs of the bond between them. Always there is a resultant intensification in the marital relationship or with extended family, and it behooves the therapist to examine these shifts for dysfunction. Often a judgment must be made whether the adolescent should be given free rein since the behavior is a move toward health, or be taken in tow like a preadolescent since the behavior is too extreme. Guidelines here are twofold: (a) Judging from the family pattern before complaints, is the adolescent moving toward more balance or less? If the parent-child relationship was extremely intense before, decreasing intensity can be functional and some overshooting of the mark can be expected. (b) Is the adolescent still in contact with the family or in danger of losing contact completely? The latter calls for retrieving action.

When the adolescent is increasing intensity, it is often done with anger, and it is a great challenge for family members to see the positive aspects rather than reject all assertions out of hand. Again, process judgments have to be made by the therapist. Is the adolescent detriangulating himself or shifting from an overintense parent relationship to the less intense parent relationship? If so, the move needs to be supported.[2] If the adolescent is reverting to an old pattern after difficulty in the outside world, it must be discouraged.

Whether the adolescent is moving toward or away from family, parental authority and control is always an issue. Here an assessment must be made as to the adequacy of the nurturing function, which is primary. If it is not adequate, it must be dealt with in reality terms. The most deprived children will accept control if they are clear that the parents are caring for them as well as they can under the circumstances and are distributing the family resources fairly. Among the rich, if the parents are delinquent runaways, there is no point in trying to help them control their teen until they can be more present. Once this occurs, it may be helpful to distinguish between obedience and assumption of responsibility. If a boy is to get to school on time above all, he must be awakened by someone regularly. If he is to learn to hear the alarm, he will probably have to be late or absent at times. Parents must judge which priorities take precedence at any given time. Therapists must judge whether parental priorities are consistent with the changes in process for which they are aiming. Both must learn not to attempt the impossible. The adolescent can not be monitored successfully outside the home. Classroom behavior is the domain of the school. Home behavior is the domain of the parents. As stated before, making judgments about teenage behavior may tax our wisdom strenuously. Being able to take a longitudinal view of family process, rather than relying on symptoms alone or a mental status check, helps immeasurably here. Nonetheless, it is important that we be humble and are prepared to be wrong. A frequent mistake is to go along with the family's assessment of health (usually based on symptoms). Bear in mind that change is always stressful and viewed by

[2]Often, the marital relationship must be realigned in order for the adolescent to become part of a balanced mobile, threesome. An example of this process is depicted in detail in the videotape "Down on Jack Night" (5).

people as a threat. In some instances, if the parents are told firmly that they have "a normal teenager" on their hands, nature takes care of the rest. Sometimes it is helpful to establish a "checkup" relationship with a family so that such judgments can be periodically reassessed.

## Symptomatic Behavior of a Sibling

The onset of symtomatic behavior of a younger sibling is frequently a moment in the life cycle of the family when a therapist has the opportunity to be truly preventive. The pattern is generally not yet entrenched. Most often, the younger sibling has become the focus of parental attention, owing to withdrawal of the eldest. The degree of withdrawal of the eldest should be evaluated. If it appears reasonable, as, for example, when an eldest goes to college while maintaining contact, leave it alone. If it is unsound with danger of loss of contact, an attempt to retrieve the eldest should be made. This is not only for the sake of the eldest, but also to reduce the intensity of the parent – younger sibling relationship, which may be all the intervention the younger sibling needs. If the eldest is left alone, then other strategies must be used. If the younger is triangulated by the parents, then one must either help the youngster talk for self vis-à-vis the parents or usurp the place of the youngster by dealing directly with the parents, which could result in the parents attempting to triangulate around the therapist. If the younger sibling is too intensely involved with one parent, increasing involvement with the other parent is the best strategy.

## Symptoms in a Parent and a Marital Problem:
## A Case Example

I will now offer in some detail an account of a family that presented as a combination of symptoms in a parent and a marital problem and required effort with three generations for a successful conclusion. Although the mother labeled herself as the problem initially, she immediately pointed to her husband and marriage as a cause. Energetic exploration further revealed the difficulties to be initiated by adolescent shifting of a delicate three-generation balance. In my judgment, this situation is much more typical than hitherto supposed. We are so used to thinking of adolescence as a time of turmoil, and the families that complain about their adolescent members are such a commonplace, that even family therapists do not generally look for the adolescent effect if a family presents with symptoms in an adult or with marital problems. Moreover, many parents are reluctant to bring in their adolescents, particularly those who are well-functioning or striving toward a more healthy adaptation. From the point of view of preventive therapy, to accept a marital problem as simply that is often a lost opportunity.

A woman in her late thirties called because she was "depressed." In tears she explained at the first session that she could no longer take her husband's anger. He shouted at her for minor transgressions like not making the tea right and gave her the "silent treatment" for a week at a time if she dared to fight back. The story this pretty but frightened woman told was that she had gone from an unhappy home into an unhappy marriage fifteen years before. Her husband, a hardworking professional, had always been demanding, cold, and insensitive to her needs. She had always catered to him and "made the best of it," taking solace in the material comforts she had and "not feeling strong enough to go it alone." When questioned about the courtship, our patient described it as a whirlwind romance during which her husband-to-be pursued her vigorously, worshipped her and even kissed her feet. She did not bargain for the fact that after marriage her husband would consciously and deliberately demand the same behavior of her in return.

During the first two years of their marriage, the husband was in the armed forces and traveled frequently, establishing an early pattern of alternating extremes of intensity. This allowed the couple to sweep their conflicts under the rug and lessened the tension. In addition, pregnancy occurred before the end of the first year and the wife became preoccupied with herself and the child, a girl. Two years later, after the husband was discharged from service, a boy was born simultaneously with husband's intense preoccupation with his own career.

So far so good. All pointed to the necessity for keeping the intensity of the marital relationship optimal. But what went wrong? The woman could give no clues. She was very happy with her children and was sure they had no problems. The girl, now thirteen, was blinking a bit and somewhat irritable lately, but that didn't seem important. The maternal grandmother, it was revealed upon inquiry, was always somewhat of a problem, but no different lately. She had been widowed when our initial patient first entered school, now lived alone and made constant demands upon the patient for services. Moreover, husband never liked his mother-in-law, clashed with her and avoided her as much as possible. The patient felt caught between them and couldn't understand why her husband didn't put himself out for her mother the way she did for his parents. She asked me if I agreed that that was selfish and unfair, and I said I was more interested in finding solutions than in making judgments. I asked for an example, preferably in the future, of the kind of difficulty this situation might cause. It turned out that the next week there was to be a family gathering, to which her mother wanted to be transported. This would mean considerable traveling out of the way for the patient and her husband, and she was certain he would object. On the other hand, she had already promised to take her mother, did not object to the traveling herself and really wanted her mother to attend. The gathering was in honor of the patient's older brother, who was visiting from out of town for a few days and was at the home of the eldest brother. These brothers, eight and ten years older than the patient, had been quite devoted to their little sister as youngsters, but were frequently at loggerheads with their mother and now had little to do with her. The patient admitted to some resentment that her brothers did not offer to transport her mother (and her mother would not ask them), but she accepted her role of being in the middle here as inevitable and viewed it as no longer important, since it occurred so rarely now. Here, then, was the original triangulation process, which was being repeated in the nuclear family. (Figure 7.7).

Still, there was no clue as to what rocked the boat. I contented myself with suggesting to the patient that she tell her husband that she wanted to take her mother to the party, and that it would be perfectly all right with her if he demurred and either went separately or didn't attend. She agreed willingly, although she didn't want to "make a habit" of doing things herself. I then told her I wanted to see her husband with her and, when she told me the usual "he won't come because he says there's nothing wrong with him," I instructed her to ask him to help with her treatment. She readily agreed, but expressed the opinion that it would make no difference.

The next day, the patient called, surprised and hesitant. She reported that her husband agreed to come in, but she thought it might not be worthwhile since he would be "on his best behavior in front of a psychiatrist." I congratulated her on her effectiveness and set a date for two weeks hence. In person, the husband was blandly intellectual and waxed expansive on "the reasoning" behind all the behavior to which his wife objected. He tended to hog the scene and, when his wife interjected occasionally, he would gesture in a brushing way with the side of his hand toward his wife's face and say, "That's not the issue." He would continue his monologue, and she would lapse into silence. He informed me that he was delighted that his wife elected to go into treatment, since he had advised her to do so ten years ago, but she had refused. He was also glad to give me any infor-

Figure 7.7

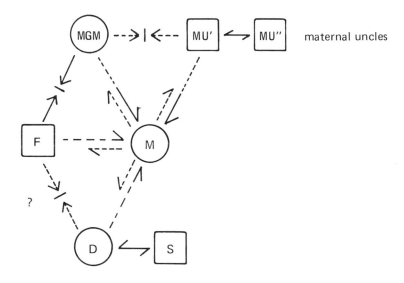

Mother is triangulated (by being a placater and rendering services) originally between siblings and mother, now primarily between mother and husband. Hypothetically, at this point in the case history she is, at times, between father and children.

mation I needed, reckoned it would take about one session and then I could continue with his wife until such time as I might need him again. He was a very reasonable man, he proclaimed, totally devoted to his family, but the way his wife was needling him and screaming lately was intolerable and he would chuck the marriage if it continued. He was launching into a convoluted theory of his wife's "neurosis" when I interrupted to ask how he had handled his wife's wanting to transport her mother to his brother-in-law's party. Both husband and wife were surprised at this, having attached no importance to it, and could barely remember what happened except that the husband did pick up mother-in-law and return her. To his comment, "I generally do," she retorted, "This is the first time without anger!" Next came a lively discussion about each other's mother, each other's personality, each other as parents, and finally the children, particularly the girl. I functioned as a switchboard, having each one talk to me in turn, insisting that the wife respond and the husband not interrupt. Often I repeated the wife's statements when the husband would go off on a tangent.

It was clear that husband and wife tended to relate to me as if I were the maternal grandmother; that is to say, they behaved in their customary manner with significant others, in this instance someone in whom they invested authority. The husband tended to compete with me as the expert, and the wife tended to submit to both of us, while encouraging us to regard her as the patient and debate over what was best for her. This process replicated the wife's original family in that she often had elicited the aid of her big brother against her mother. It also replicated the husband's original family, in that his mother often reprimanded him as a youngster for his condescending attitude towards his father. The husband would also engage his mother by defending his younger sister against her authority. In this session, to some extent I went along with the pattern, allowing the husband to speak his piece and responding to some of the wife's pleas for direction. As the session progressed, I tended more and more to assert my responsibility for the conduct of the therapy, declining to debate with the husband and insisting that the wife voice her objections more directly toward him (Figure 7.8). The couple accommodated to me, but were unable to maintain a more balanced interaction between themselves for more than a minute or two without my intervention. I therefore made the judgment that I needed more of a therapeutic handle and proceeded to explore further.

What had emerged was that the predominant pattern had

Figure 7.8

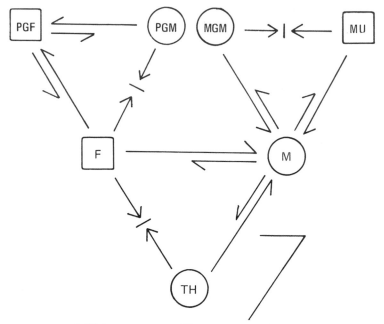

Initial engagement: Therapy system is
mirror image of both parents' original system.

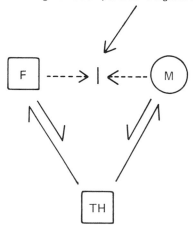

As therapist takes
control intermittent
open conflict develops
between parents.

been repeated early in the marriage, when the couple lived with the husband's parents and the paternal grandmother tended to admonish the husband for not paying enough attention to his wife at times. After the couple moved into a home of their own, the maternal mother-in-law became more involved with the wife, and the husband would periodically fight with her or make demands on the wife when he deemed mother-in-law to be "taking over too much." In recent months, however, he had simply been withdrawing from the field, "tired of fighting," as he saw it. The wife saw it as abandonment and part of his "sickness," an increasing preoccupation with religion. In mentioning this during a heated exchange, the wife threw in for good measure that the husband was imposing his religious practices on their daughter and "turning daughter against mother." The husband retorted that he had imposed nothing; rather, it was the daughter who had challenged him to practice what he preached, and it was "after finding her arguments sound" that he had embarked upon an intense study of his religion. I saw that his behavior mimicked the intensely studious days of this man's youth under the guidance of his ambitious mother and, by insisting on details about the daughter, I was finally able to enlarge my understanding of what had transpired in this family.

In her preteen years, the daughter had been more involved with the wife than the husband, tending to be solicitous and directive toward the former and noncommunicative with the latter. She thus functioned similarly to the maternal grandmother, and there was a reciprocal relationship between the intensity of the daughter-mother relationship and that of the mother-grandmother relationship. After the daughter became a teenager, she became increasingly friendly with neighboring teenagers who attended a parochial school, spent time with their families, and developed an interest in their customs. This became the issue around which she began to communicate with her father. At first, she pointed to inconsistencies between father's proclaimed beliefs and actions. Next, they engaged in long discussions, and eventually, father became very active in the house of worship and both children entered parochial shcool. At the same time, daughter began to pull away from mother and rejected mother's pursuits. Occasionally, there were open clashes, and mother accused father of enjoying daughter's "freshness." Father withdrew further from mother, and mother found herself appealing more and more to grandmother. Grandmother, in turn, inveighed against father and daughter and then proceeded to make more and more demands on our unhappy mother (Figure 7.9).

We were all able to agree that mother needed to learn how to handle her own mother and I told the father that we needed his help in this effort. He was to encourage his wife but not get involved with grandmother himself and, at all costs, he must not fight his wife's battles for her. I specifically requested that he return with three examples of how his mother-in-law interfered with his household or imposed on his wife, so that we could formulate tactics. The husband thought this "very reasonable." I was eager to bring in the children, but both parents could see "little purpose" in this idea, so I bided my time.

Sure enough, two weeks later mother reported that just the day before, daughter had "opened up a vile mouth" to her for the first time and she, mother, was overwhelmed and distraught. To make matters worse, her husband was present

Figure 7.9

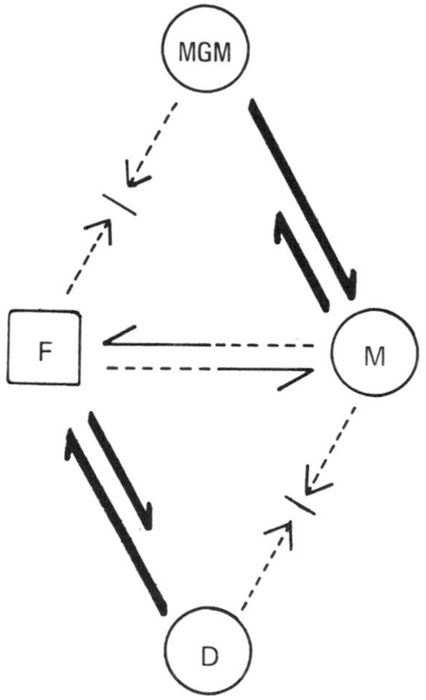

As daughter shifts from underfunctioning with mother to intense over-functioning with father, marital relationship becomes less intense and mother falls back on her mother intensely.

and seemed to laugh. "Shouldn't he, in a case like this, make his daughter apologize to me?" she pleaded. I responded by saying that I believed mother could learn how to handle daughter competently and, indeed, she had done well by condemning daughter's language and refusing to further discuss the minor issue involved. Moreover, I commended father for "refraining from interfering." Father denied laughing and pointed out that there wasn't much room for him, since grandmother happened to be on the telephone with mother at the same time threatening to break granddaughter's arm if she spoke to mother like that again. One couldn't ask for a better example of child and grandparent relating as peers over an underfunctioning parent. Daughter also related to father as *his* mother, let us remember, and father confirmed this by blurting out that daughter told him not to let the psychiatrist get the idea that she was brainwashed by father. I quickly pointed out that this was a message that daughter had a few things to say and she ought to have the right to speak for herself. Both parents agreed somewhat reluctantly to bring in the children, and the rest of the time was devoted to husband's homework and giving guidelines to the wife on how she might assert herself with her mother in a useful way.

In the fourth session, two weeks later, both children appeared friendly and interested, the boy clearly allied with and supportive of his older sister. In response to my query, mother reported that daughter had come to her on her own the day after our last session to apologize. I praised the daughter and suggested that mother thank father for his wisdom in allowing mother and daughter to work things out for themselves. Mother did so and also complimented me for helping them, saying that her husband had been much "nicer." He refused this left-handed compliment, attributing his even-temperedness to less tension at work and hinting that in the future he might erupt again. I midly observed that he had turned something positive into a negative and daughter chimed in that he was very critical. She recounted how she had looked up to him because he seemed so much stronger than mother, and also stated that she couldn't stand mother's intrusiveness. When she called her father a hypocrite regarding religion, he seemed to take it very well and actually did something about it, earning her respect and affection. Now, however, he had become the expert and was constantly criticizing her and demanding that she be ever more exact in her religious observances. She was beginning to think that father was just as bad as mother in his own way. She loved them both but there were problems with both. Here was a good point on the pendulum swing between mother and father from which to work. It turned out that daughter was very upset herself. She had a pronounced tic as she told of her despair at "getting mother to understand" her bid for more freedom. Turning to father had some merits but was no substitute. And grandmother was something else lately! Brother had similar gripes on a lesser scale. Mother had been "fussing" at him more lately since sister was with father, and grandma, too, had become much more concerned about his clothes and manners. Brother was slated to take sister's place were she to withdraw. Both parents were struck by this appeal from their children and listened attentively, their own cyclical debate forgotten. We were in business. From this point on, the therapy proceeded apace. I kept a watchful eye on the balance in the nuclear family by including the children from time to time and giving guidance to the parents, while both of them proceeded to renegotiate relationships with their respective parents.

My strategy, derived from my understanding of the total family organization, was to increase interaction between mother and daughter while maintaining contact with father and daughter. This tended to deintensify the mother-grandmother relationship so that mother could learn to assert herself in a functional way with husband's cooperation. Eventually, husband would work on the relationship with *his* mother and the wife would cooperate in this venture. In order to achieve these ends, two types of dysfunctional processes had to be constantly monitored and corrected. One was the tendency of mother and father to underfunction and overfunction respectively vis-à-vis daughter, maternal grandmother and each other. Such tendencies lead to too much or too little interaction and hence promote instability. The second was the tendency to triangulate. This family exhibited what I have called the pattern of shifting triangles: Mother and father debated about their daughter and respective mothers; mother and daughter looked to father for judgments about their relationship; and father and daughter often communicated through mother (Figure 7.10). It is necessary to detriangulate each relationship in order for it to be renegotiated.

Some therapists work on the marital relationship exclusively, while others direct their attention to the extended fam-

Figure 7.10

Shifts in the Triangulation Pattern

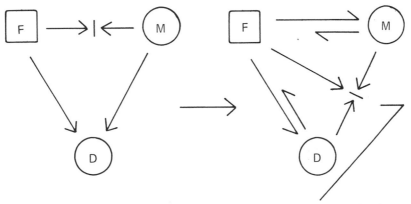

Father and mother argue over daughter.

Father disrupts mother-daughter conflict by playing judge.

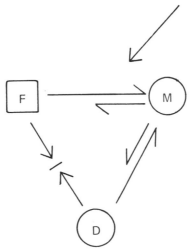

Mother gives messages to father from daughter and to daughter from father.

ily in the belief that this will decrease the tension in the nuclear family and the rest will take care of itself. My experience has convinced me that, especially in the case of the family with adolescents, active attention to both nuclear and extended families is more efficient, more widely applicable, and less dangerous. For me, it is more fun.

In the above illustration, relieving some of mother's anxiety about husband and daughter increased her feeling of competence and lent impetus to her resolve to "learn how to be a whole person with her mother." More important, reinvolvement of mother with her husband and daughter was a fast way of deintensifying the mother-grandmother relationship. Had mother been pushed to "become a self" with her mother too early, it might have resulted in useless confrontations requiring more difficult fresh starts or even in destructive explosions. True, this would be due to poor clinical judgment rather than to a fault of the method, but I have seen major errors of this kind in the best hands. My point is that it is generally easier to make judgments when all parties are seen. (Grandmother was brought in "live" at one point during the course of treatment.) One of the best tactics for detriangulation is still to have all three parties present and to encourage all three to speak for themselves. This does not mean that the therapist is taking over family functions any more than a football coach is kicking and passing when watching a game; but he surely can spot the problems faster than when being told about the game.

The method I have described is more widely applicable because many families and individuals are not well enough put together to carry out tasks on their own, particularly when it comes to dealing with their family of origin. I firmly believe that the ultimate payload for each and every one of us comes from learning to conduct ourselves as adults after reviving childhood patterns with our original family. I am not willing, however, to consign those who are unable or unwilling to do it to the therapeutic ashheap. When much of the dysfunction remains with the extended family, the children may be better integrated than their parents and therefore a source of strength for the family. Not utilizing such strength is a waste. Adolescents frequently make good therapeutic allies.

Finally, to focus only on the marriage and/or the extended families, if successful, necessarily means decreasing the intensity of parent-child relationship and increasing the anxiety of the child. Adolescents don't generally sit still under these conditions and I have, unfortunately, seen many destructive acts and suicide attempts on the part of adolescents when the therapist ignored them. It is not necessary and sometimes not humane to do so.

The opening phases of the above example demonstrate that, although the principles are simple, the nuances of language and the subtleties of behavior may confound understanding. For instance, the wife reported that the clashes with her husband were most disturbing, but it was my judgment that the overall decrease in interaction precipitated the clashes. Later, the woman admitted to feeling excluded by husband and daughter. Both parents tended to downplay the role of the daughter, and this had to be energetically investigated. The decision to facilitate mother-daughter interaction was made not only to balance the intensity between both parents, but because it was deemed that, despite their difficulties, mother and daughter were the most well-functioning pair. Had father been as flexible as he claimed, I might have chosen to focus at first on the father-daughter relationship and father's extended family.

## General Considerations of Treatment

In many instances, one parent-child relationship is so intense or "toxic" that deintensification is a must. Generally, the parent involved is only too willing to "take a vacation" (at least temporarily), and the other parent will agree to take over responsibility, having been critical of the other parent anyway and not really knowing first-hand what the water feels like. Here again, it is helpful to have the adolescent actively participate in the plan to shift parental responsibility.

The above considerations apply to those families where there has been some combination of shifting of the overfunctioning-underfunctioning axis of relationship with an adolescent and a shifting of intensity from one relationship to another. As already mentioned in connection with the symptomatic adolescent, the remaining possibility is that the adolescent has withdrawn from all family members. This can occur in a mild way, as in the instance of an adolescent becoming increasingly involved in a peer group yet maintaining reasonable contact with the family. This increases intensity in the parental relationship and/or parent–other-sibling relationship and may bring out some conflict or tendency toward imbalance of functioning, but in time the realignment generally becomes balanced (Figure 7.11).

At the other extreme, the adolescent may insulate himself or herself from the family by running away (literally or figuratively) or becoming totally self-absorbed. I use the term *insulation* to describe the process reciprocal to fusion, the latter being the overfunctioning-underfunctioning process carried to extremes. Fusion and insulation are truly complementary and are always, and only, present together in a family. An insulated adolescent is always avoiding either a severe triangulation process or a fusion, and the family has to compensate by fusing or triangulating elsewhere. (Figure 7.12). These families are often cut off from their extended families, and the adolescent is only replicating behavior of the grandparents. A chronic situation easily develops, and it is most difficult to treat. Such families can be treated but, in my experience, only by convening the whole family and coaching them directly how to reestablish contact, first with the adolescent and then with the extended family. Here, especially, if the adolescent is ignored, he or she may be lost forever.

# Conclusions

The various ways adolescent behavior may affect a family, as well as the major implications for future health of the family, have been outlined. The usual presentation of adolescent "with problems" has been underplayed. I hope to have given some sense of the diagnostic and therapeutic challenge that families

Figure 7.11

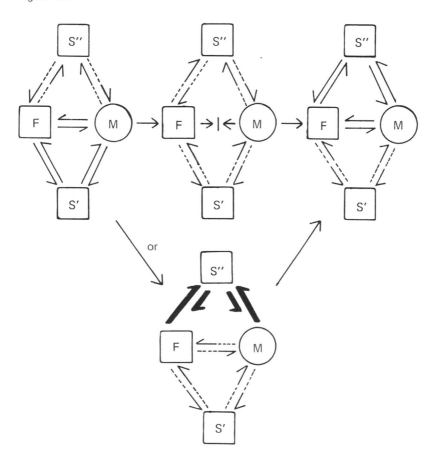

S′  = Eldest Son
S″ = Second Son

Withdrawal of eldest sibling leads to conflict between parents or intense overfunctioning of parents vis-à-vis younger sibling. Realignment may then result in balanced threesome with younger sibling and appropriately reduced intensity with eldest.

Figure 7.12

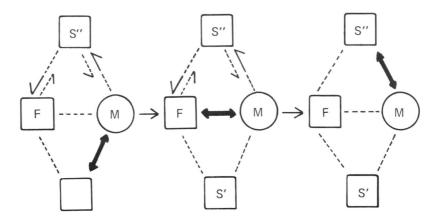

Fusion of eldest sibling with mother; insulated father; younger "well" sibling.

Insulating eldest sibling and temporary fusion of parents.

Lost eldest sibling. Fusion of mother with younger sibling.

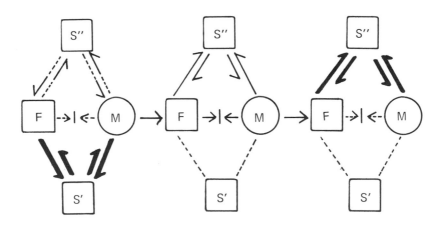

Constant triangulation of eldest sibling. Sibling two is "well sibling."

Insulation of eldest (withdrawal, runaway, psychosis) produces intensification of parental conflict and attempt to triangulate around "well sibling."

Constant triangulation around former "well sibling." Lost older sibling. Marriage less intense again.

with adolescents offer. I have implied that correct assessment of family process leads to correct therapeutic strategies, but I caution the reader to remember that diagnosis and intervention go hand in hand in family therapy. It is frequently only after false starts and unsuccessful interventions that a meaningful picture emerges. I have refrained from discussing specific tactics to be used by the therapist in pursuing the decided strategy. Tactics are, at least in part, a function of the idiosyncratic relationship between therapist and family. What works with one, may not work with another. Tactics are best learned, therefore, working with families under the tutelage of a flexible teacher who can allow the student therapist to be innovative within the framework of a consistent theory.

I think it fair to say that the attainment of adolescence by a family member always constitutes a profound landmark in the life cycle of the family, with attendant pitfalls and opportunities. Treating such families is always a challenge and may try the acumen and fortitude of the most seasoned therapist. As with the families themselves, however, if the therapist can weather the storm, the rewards can be substantial.

# References

1. Ackerman, Nathan W., "Adolescent problems: A Symptom of Family Disorder," *Family Process, 1* (2) (1962), 202-213.
2. Bell, John Elderkin, Family Group Therapy in the Treatment of Juvenile and Adult Offenders, paper read at 36th Annual Conference California Probation, Parole and Correctional Association, San Diego, Calif. (May 26, 1966), in Bell, *Family Therapy* (New York: Jason Aronson, 1975).
3. Thomas, Lewis, *Natural Man, the Lives of a Cell* (New York: Viking, 1974).
4. Papp, Peggy, (ed.), *Family Therapy Full Length Case Studies* (New York: Gardner, 1977).
5. Ackerman, Norman J., McFarlane, William, and Terkelsen, Kenneth. *"Down on Jack Night,"* videotape, (New York: Family Video Productions, 1975).

# VIII
# THE IRRELEVANCE OF STYLE IN FAMILY THERAPY

**i**t is my contention that while style is important to the individual family therapist, in that it is necessary to find the best way to use oneself in interacting with a family, outcome depends solely on the achievement of or failure to achieve balanced threesomes within the family. This can be and is accomplished in many ways by many therapists using different techniques as well as different styles. By *techniques* I mean devices, procedures, and tactics, communicable to and reproducible by other family therapists. (These will be discussed in the next chapter.) By *style* I mean, the therapist's personal qualities and manner in engaging the family. Style, then, is part of what is called the "use of self."

## Two Pioneer Family Therapists Compared

No two distinguished family therapists could appear more different in their presentation of themselves and manner than Nathan W. Ackerman and Murray Bowen. Ackerman was characterized by Lyman Wynne as a "man who created instant intimacy" (1), whereas Bowen consistently remains cordial and unemotional — in his own words, "I have spent my life avoiding transference" (2). Ackerman tends to be challenging, using emotionally loaded phrases, making highly personal statements of his own directly to individual family members, and generally eliciting intense responses, positive and negative. He can be alternately comforting and damning and uses pointed humor that is sometimes on the edge of sarcasm. He moves within the family from member to member, taking sides freely, supporting one, undercutting another, and easily reversing a moment later if he sees fit. Often he directs action in the session, moving people around the room and challenging them to confront one another in special ways. He is a man on the move. In interviews in front of an audience, he has usually drawn condemnation and admiration in equal amounts.

Bowen keeps a comfortable distance. He rarely goes after affect and generally finds a way either to forestall an outpouring or to intellectualize it. When a distraught person begins to talk of the terrible feelings he or she had this week, he may ask how many times out of ten they were successful in not reacting. He makes few personal statements directly to others: that is to say, he usually does not reveal his own affect or beliefs regarding an individual. When someone makes a personal statement about him, he may nod or chuckle affably but he does not counter. Generally, he addresses each member individually and discourages interaction among family members. He gathers information in an organized way, focusing on what goes on outside the session; suggests ideal ways a person might react and respond to other family members; and coaches people in taking initiatives in changing their way of relating to members of their extended families. Rarely do family members react to him with intensity or challenge him. His audiences may be intellectually approving or puzzled.

Despite these extreme differences, Ackerman and Bowen often achieve the same ends with a family, not only by using different strategies, but sometimes by using the identical strategy.[1] In these instances, the process within the session can be described in identical terms, as in the following examples.

## An Example of Treatment by Nathan W. Ackerman

A family was presented to Ackerman by a therapist who deemed them impossible to move and wanted to give up (3). After a consultation, Ackerman judged the family to be workable and tried to persuade the therapist to continue along other lines. The therapist, however, demurred. It was finally decided that Ackerman would see the family for six sessions to test his clinical hunch, and then the family, if this was indicated, would be treated by someone else. The family agreed to this procedure, which was dictated by many circumstances having nothing to do with the family's problems or needs.

Indeed, it was difficult to focus on a particular problem. No sooner did Ackerman begin to explore one area than another issue forcibly intruded itself. No sooner was one person addressed than another disrupted. Although there were three children, all of whom displayed various symptoms, the parents, particularly the mother, seemed to be concerned with the eldest, a boy of fourteen. Mother complained of his freshness and rebelliousness, and father complained of his academic failures. When Ackerman tried to elicit details, the boy denied all and the parents evaded by blaming themselves, alluding to marital problems that couldn't be discussed in front of the children.

Ackerman is generally an expert at discussing anything in front of children, but these parents adroitly managed to drag in the obviously sensitive and shy middle boy of eleven, who obediently agreed to his need to talk to the doctor. Attempts to engage the boy directly led to confusion and more withdrawal on the part of the boy, and to charming but disruptive

[1]By strategy I mean the general long-range path of altering the family process. It may be conscious or unconscious.

comments from the youngest, a girl of seven. Turning his attention to her, Ackerman got no further as she coyly flirted but offered no comments about herself or her family and ignored all questions. The parents beamed. All in all, it was a rather remarkable display of family solidarity, and Ackerman appeared to strike out in the first session.

In the second session, Ackerman homed in on the parents, individually and separately. He explored present and past, always evoking much feeling. The father was quite willing to share his sadness about his failure to achieve his ambition and his fears regarding a heart illness. Mother equally opened up about her frustrations and disappointments in her status and in her sexual life. Both had had very difficult upbringings and suffered severe hardships. The marital relationship, however, remained obscure. The parents never addressed one another, and on many occasions when they made eye contact and looked as if they might, the eldest boy would interject with an irrelevancy. Ackerman repeatedly had to gently stop the boy from distracting. This was difficult, because often the parents would try to follow the boy's change in topic.

Ackerman persisted and, after many allusions by the parents to difficulties that could not be discussed in front of the children, it was agreed to meet without the children. Immediately on sitting down in the third session, both parents began to complain about the eldest son, who had been particularly aggressive during the week. With much tenacity, Ackerman elicited the bare outline of a sexual problem. The woman was not orgastic and had little or no desire, and the man was frustrated but for the most part had given up pursuing. Their sexual life was like their emotional life — distant and mechanical.

Their relationship was also potentially explosive, however, and attempts to open up communications between the pair directly were aborted. Hints of bitterness and rage on both parts quickly faded into meaningless intellectual explanations and silence. Finally, Ackerman began to move in on both of them in turn. He made many statements regarding his own affect, challenging the man to rouse himself from his lethargy and "stick out his manhood," at the same time encouraging the woman to relax, trust him, and "let things flow." Many body movements and gestures were used deliberately to dramatize these expressions. He condemned the man's weak withdrawal, even while sympathizing with his fears, and pointed to himself as having coped with fears by taking chances. He disapproved of the woman's suspicious hiding, yet supported her right to unhappy tears. He expressed his own frustration with them again and again, and finally sat back, saying he was working too hard, and waited for them to come to him. There seemed to be some response at the end of the session, if one looked closely. The man brightened a little and the woman softened, but this seemed small recompense for all the effort.

In the fourth session, however, both husband and wife agreed that Ackerman had become very important to them. They reported that they had talked quite a bit about Ackerman and the sessions. Each spoke much more sympathetically about the other and there were a few expressions of tenderness. No mention was made of the children. Ackerman continued to relate directly to each in turn, again constantly using expressions of his own feeling to encourage "opening up" and discourage "hiding." In this session, the development of the relationship was explored, with heavy emphasis on the positive aspects of the courtship and the occasions when they were alone. Many of their negative reactions to one another were connected by Ackerman with their experiences in their original families. In turn, parallels were made with their reactions to Ackerman in the first three sessions.

In the fifth session, the wife reported having an orgasm with her husband during the week. The emotional atmosphere was warm, and husband and wife talked directly with one another for the first time. Ackerman was very approving but cautioned them about forgetting about the children altogether in their quest for romance, saying that the real trick would be to maintain their relationship while dealing with the children. In the sixth session both husband and wife expressed fear that without Ackerman they would revert back to where they had been. Ackerman reassured them that they could keep it up, that other help was available, and that they had much work to do yet with the children, particularly the eldest boy. After some expressions of sadness at parting they bid farewell.

## An Example of Treatment by Murray Bowen

Let us now look at an example of Bowen's work (4). In this example,[2] Bowen is working with a couple in the presence of two other couples who, in turn, will be interviewed by him in the presence of the others. No interaction is allowed between one couple and another, whether in or out of the group; nor does Bowen have any exchange with a couple other than the one he is interviewing. In line with his emphasis on the cognitive, Bowen's rationale for having other couples present is that "families learn from each other," especially if one can "preserve the emotional separateness... necessary for working out... family process between spouses" (5).

It is evident from the interviews, however, that the couple being interviewed are very much aware of the other couples as an audience and associate them with Bowen. For example, at a time when husband and wife are vying with each other in an apparent attempt to set Bowen up as a judge of the best patient, the husband says, "How can you lie in front of this group?" Thus, the couple or family in question relate to the other couples as if they were allied with the therapist. Because the other couples must remain silent, this is never subject to

[2]Although this discussion relies partly on the manuscript in van den Blink's book, I did see the original videotape of this couple at a conference. (As in supervision, I prefer to see for myself rather than be restricted to written or audio accounts.) I have better access to other videotapes of Bowen's, but this one he himself obviously thought was a good example of his work. Likewise, Ackerman, I know, was well satisfied with the just-cited example of his work. There is an added historical plus in that both examples occurred at about the same time: Bowen's in 1968; Ackerman's about 1965.

correction or modification, and every action of the therapist is given added weight and has greater impact. It makes the therapist more difficult to challenge without his having to assert himself dramatically or emotionally. (With half a dozen stalwarts at one's side, one can saunter over to a couple of hooligans snatching a purse with far greater effect than brandishing a fist alone.) It would also, in my opinion, make the therapist more significant to the family and would intensify their efforts to triangulate around him. Since this process is the *sine qua non* of successful therapy, it is no surprise to me that Bowen reports that "it was even easier for the therapist to become emotionally triangled into the families' emotional systems in this setting"; and yet, "the surprise was the unusually rapid progress"(6). Bowen explains this rapidity as solely the result of "learning from other families" and ignores the fact that his own theoretical position leads to the conclusion that the less the therapist can be "triangled in," the better for therapy. It has long been my contention that good therapists regularly participate in triangulation to varying extents and that *becoming detriangulated* is of the essence. But more about that later. The point for now is that Bowen is interacting with one couple, and that the style and process is essentially the same as it would be if he were seeing the couple alone albeit with an audience. (Ackerman saw the other couple in a setting where a camera and cameraman were behind a one-way screen.)

Two sessions will be reported here from the middle of ongoing therapy. The first session opens with one of Bowen's very few statements of feeling: "I missed you last week." (The couple had been on vacation.) Bowen might have meant, "I didn't see you," but immediately emotion is stirred, as the husband answers, "I'll bet you did!" and the wife says, "We didn't miss this!" with a nervous laugh. The husband follows up with, "You say nasty things while we are away," and then makes several other bantering sallies, baiting Bowen personally. The only retort is, "Let's report our plans."

This closing of ranks and, particularly, the rejection of a joining move of the therapist is typical of a couple that tend to fuse. The wife appears to be the "overfunctioning" or pseudoresponsible member.[3] This is borne out a moment later, when she states that it was a nice vacation, but immediately turns the floor over to her husband when Bowen presses for specifics. This pattern of wife directing Bowen to husband is repeated again and again. At times, she even suggests the topic be changed, and Bowen obeys. On several occasions when Bowen and the wife actually get to talking, the husband interrupts as the wife begins to evidence anxiety. The husband is an expert at talking about things. When he does get close to talking about himself, the wife distracts or the husband focuses on the wife or son.

Both spouses evade by debating and engaging in digs at each other. They are clearly "hooked in" to one another. (At one point, the husband gives a strikingly clear description of an element of fusion: "When she is upset, regardless of what she is upset about, then I sorta get into it, even if there is no verbalization, we are sort of communicating her upset inside me.") Bowen, with infinite patience and aplomb, ignores all this and constantly sticks to business ("Mr. X, you say there has been a little progress. If you were to specify it, what would it be?" or "What are your thoughts about the disengaging efforts, Mrs. X?"). When personal comments are directed toward Bowen, he is a bobbing and weaving soft-shoe dancer, appearing to effortlessly avoid arrows and bouquets alike as they come hurling at him.

Husband and wife both agree that the tension they experienced during the previous week was due to the husband's conflict with the son, and he launches into a tedious monologue about it. This is an avoidance of Bowen's question and an attempt to triangulate with Bowen about the son. The monotony is broken only by an occasional skirmish between the spouses, starting with the wife's interrupting to disagree with some minor details. We learn that the husband has always

---

[3]The distinction between "overfunctioner" and "underfunctioner" is often unclear in that it may vary from time to time, place to place and in different areas of functioning at the same time. It is also of little import because neither party is assuming true responsibility and if one becomes responsible, the other will also.

been the good boy and conformer in his family of origin and that he "gets into a position of inflexibility" with his son. The wife tends to get in the middle. She also has more authority over the son than the husband. This week, however, he stayed calm with his son and the son obeyed him.

At the end of the monologue, Bowen asks blandly, "Have you made any progress?" Again, the husband triangulates, this time speculating about his "satyriasis obsession." Bowen asks if "this kind of thinking is profitable." Over and over, Bowen asks about progress. Finally, the husband picks up the reference to the work of the therapeutic system, but the best he can do is say, "We can talk about the kids a little bit, without getting too emotional." He attributes the change to his wife's not taking it "as seriously as she used." When pressed further, he ends up lamely saying he doesn't really know and suggests his wife talk about it.

When Bowen accepts this and questions her about "disengagement" from each other, she adroitly baits her husband by referring to his "defensiveness" about his fantasies of other women. This leads to a debate over who is "disengaging" best. The wife points out she stayed out of the argument between father and son, although she was tempted to join the son. There are several direct attempts to involve Bowen. Bowen ducks with humorous reversal: To the wife's assertion that she is disengaging "just like you said" he replies, "I recommended something like that?" "this is absolutely foreign to me!" and "I am in favor of all this togetherness and people being nice to each other."

Note that these remarks not only keep Bowen disengaged but are also specific refusals to accept "blame" for the wife's actions. She is actually proferring a pseudoresponsible relationship. Unlike the relationship between Bowen and husband, Bowen and wife know exactly what each other is talking about all the time. Bowen manages to stay out, but the debate goes on...and on...and on. Bowen makes one or two more attempts to get the wife to talk about herself; she turns it over to her husband, who triangulates about his symptoms, only to return to debating with his wife over the therapeutic process itself. Bowen makes no comment and turns to the next couple.

He appears to have gotten nowhere. The fact that his nearly fused couple engages in mild triangulation around Bowen is, however, a move toward health.

A week later, there is an immediate change of tactics on Bowen's part as he asks the husband if the wife changed. The husband picks up on this for a while, as curiously enough, his concern about his wife's fears come across with more meaning than when he talks about his own symptoms; there is even some semblance of a tender interchange between spouses. When, however, Bowen asks, "How did you flip her?" referring to her improvement, the husband denies all responsibility. He then describes his "accepting" his wife's "distance" and her discussing fears of her own "for the first time" — indicating a shift toward balance. The wife had found some lumps in her armpit (which subsequently disappeared). This brings up the subject of death, and the husband immediately starts the pattern going: He tries to address the other couple, is cut off by Bowen, then goes back to his own symptoms, stressing his progress and injecting some humor. Bowen is johnny-on-the-spot and picks up on the *personal* fragment in a long-winded discourse on stomach. When the husband says, "I thought you might like to talk about change," Bowen interrupts with, "The biggest change of all is your sense of humor about it!" and chuckles. This is a personal response and the first direct interaction between Bowen and husband, a breakthrough of the barricade.

The course of things changes from here on. The husband goes on to talk meaningfully about his reacting to his wife and compliments her on her current behavior. She takes it as an insult about the past, however, and interrupts to debate. This time, the husband drops it and returns to Bowen to continue talking about his new-found freedom from conforming to his wife's expectations. Now, Bowen himself reverts to the old pattern of wife getting in the middle and addresses the wife for an unproductive exchange; this time, the husband brings Bowen back with a cogent statement about himself followed by a personal statement to Bowen: "I think what's really happening is, the more unorthodox my personal behavior, the more comfortable I become. (Pause.) That may be a gem, I know he is writing it down!" And Bowen responds personally again: "You know I was thinking, if unorthodox is a goal and how about, you know, how about this going unorthodox, you know, and get this show on the road!" Now the husband warms to the subject and talks at length of how he would like to get out of his "box." He talks poignantly and determinedly, taking responsibility for himself: "Maybe it's my own box I've put myself in." At one point he mentions, "I think I mentioned threats and threatened last time, which you also wrote down." Then, "making threats and being threatened still make me anxious."

That Bowen is strongly and personally relating to this man now is borne out, in my judgment, by the fact that, although this comment is a parenthetical aside, the next comment Bowen makes much later is, "What kind of, how are you working on this, Mr. X, this thing of threatening and being threatened?" A moment later Bowen returns to his original tack of asking husband about wife and presses it. This prevents too much closeness with husband, reverses the more predominant pattern of wife talking about husband, gives wife a chance to hear something about herself, runs into the ground the notion that husband knows everything about wife, and eventually elicits "I" statements.

It is much easier to work with husband about wife than approach wife directly. This is an accommodation to the family system of wife as triangled member. Husband makes several meaningful explications of the interaction between his wife and himself when Bowen brings the discussion back to the wife's reaction to his stomach symptoms. This the wife cannot resist, and she jumps in for her share of the action, again mentioning an interchange that had occurred between her and Bowen in the previous session. This is important, because it demonstrates that Bowen has become a significant other to her also. She goes on to talk in a rambling, disconnected way of "change," mimicking husband's successful response to Bowen's pushing for progress, and she mentions "good feelings," referring to the relationship with husband. Bowen does not pick up on this one; rather he asks about her "cancer scare." I would deem this an error partly due to the wife's disjunctive, rapid-fire communications and partly due to Bowen's greater difficulty in responding personally to her.

In any case, this relationship does not flow like the one with the husband does. Instantly, the husband disrupts by engaging the wife in a military diversion regarding the changing of her will. This works very well, and the wife ambles back to her "good feelings" with her husband. For the most part, she attributes them to her husband rather than herself; nonetheless, she is positive about her husband and for the first time gives him legitimate credit for his efforts. The husband doesn't acknowledge the compliment, but tries to start another debate by suggesting that wife maintain her good feelings when it comes to bedroom matters.

This time the wife responds clearly and cites a recent example of her doing exactly that. Moreover, as Bowen apparently prepares to call time, she insists on "just one more thing." She refers this time in detail to her thoughts about her husband's "fantasizing about other women," finally stating, "I realized that this was fantasizing on my part" (that is, imagining that the husband's fantasies occurred while they were making love) "and I came around to realize that it's at other times [that he's doing it] and... it suddenly dropped away." This is the most differentiating statement the woman has made. Bowen replies with his fourth personal statement: "I hear you on that one!"

### Discussion of the Cited Examples

The Ackerman sessions are distinguished by numerous personal statements made by him to each spouse. Other outstanding features are Ackerman's repeatedly going after affect, use of his own affect, and pointed confrontations—as opposed to Bowen's low-keyed avoidance of emotion. Both men use humor extensively, but Ackerman's is earthy and almost always in the service of promoting interchange (particularly interchange of affect), whereas Bowen uses humor to distract from interchange when it gets too heated or to avoid personal reactions of his own. Ackerman seems never to shrink from personal response, but he shuns the intellectual ones; Bowen encourages and actively elicits "thinking about" process. Ackerman constantly makes deliberate use of his own and the family's nonverbal communications, in particular, their body language. I have never seen Bowen do this. Ackerman constantly strives for more contact and closeness, between himself and patients as well as between patients; Bowen keeps his distance and encourages others to do likewise.

How can I say these two therapists do the same thing? It is simply that style has relatively little to do with process. Style is often a matter of how much or how, whereas process is a matter of what. One can be more or less loud, dramatic, emotive, intellectual, verbal, active, mobile, physical, bizarre, and much else, while still engaging in the same process. Process has to do with questions such as these: Is one relating to a family? Which part of the family? Is the relationship balanced, imbalanced, or barricaded? Has one been triangulated? Is one insulated from one member or fused with another, or both? The artistry of Ackerman is that he can become very emotive and not fuse. The artistry of Bowen is that he can almost totally avoid emotion without insulating. Even when Ackerman overreacts — as he did in an example offered by van den Blink (7) — he manages to regain balance quickly. Even when Bowen cuts off a person (as he did the wife in this interview), he manages to retrieve contact moments later. The mark of a true champion is twofold: (a) to be able to do exactly the wrong thing at exactly the right time; and (b) to forget one's mistakes instantly.

In these interviews both therapists appear to get nowhere fast, initially. Actually, they are very busy avoiding triangulation and subtly enhancing their significant otherness. Both therapists attempt, unsuccessfully, to elicit explications of self from both spouses. Both are thwarted by the family maneuvers to prevent a balanced relationship with the therapist. Both can do little with the intense distortion of the spouse relationship. Both take strong "I positions." Both form balanced relationships of their own with parts of the family system. Both end up with a working threesome.

Ackerman starts with a family in which tremendous conflict between spouses is covered by distance. Distance is maintained by triangulating over the son. Ackerman usurps the son's place, and establishes a balanced relationship with each spouse, and there is miraculous opening up of the relationship between spouses (Figure 8.1).

In Bowen's family, the couple exhibit a pseudoresponsible relationship and a pattern of triangulation about the wife, who acts as mediator and who controls the son better than her husband does. The relationship between husband and son is barricaded. Again, Bowen occupies the same position as the son (who probably replicates that of the grandfather) and establishes a balanced relationship with the husband after refusing the "underfunctioning" or nonresponsible overreactive position the wife offers him. As the husband and Bowen break through their barricade, almost magically, the wife takes responsibility for self with Bowen and refers positively to her husband (Figure 8.2).

## The Evolution of Family Therapy Transcends Style

It is instructive to look at Murray Bowen's own account of his evolution (8, 9). In 1954 he began observing whole families on a hospital ward, making many new observations but not knowing what to do with them, although he knew "within six months" that "some method of therapy for family members together was indicated." By 1957, many patterns had been charted, including "interdependent triads" (9), but he had great difficulty in handling them: "The parents would focus so much on details about the child's problem that it was difficult to maintain sufficient focus on the parental relationship." In these early days, "there was strong emphasis on analyzing the intrapsychic process in each spouse in the presence of the other spouse" (8). Gradually, intrapsychic process was deemphasized, and in 1960 Bowen began to exclude the children, and "spouses were encouraged to speak directly to each other" with direct expression of feeling" (8).

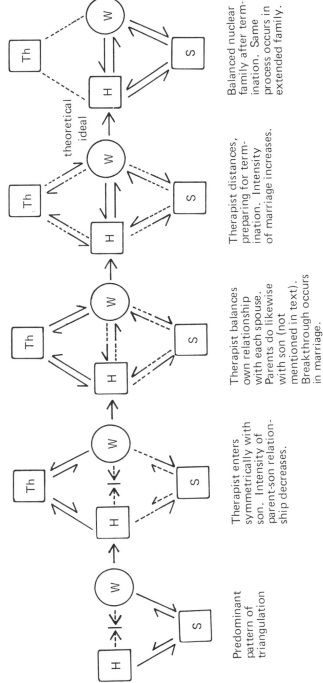

Figure 8.1

Figure 8.2

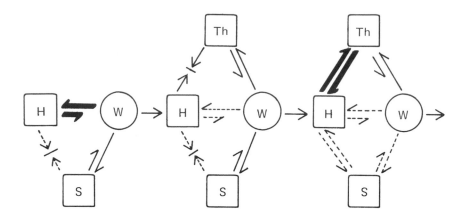

Predominant
pattern of
triangulation

Therapist enters
symmetrically
with son. Intensity
of marital relation-
ship decreases.

Therapist breaks
through with
husband and
moves closer.
Husband does
same with son
as wife distances
from son.

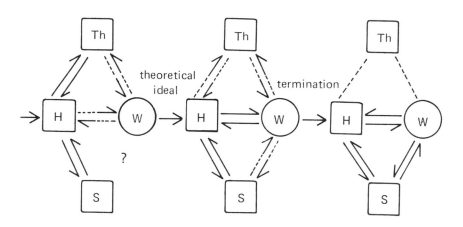

As therapist and
wife balance
relationship, so
do husband and
wife. Theoreti-
cally, wife and
son do too (but
no data available).

Therapist
decreases intensity
with husband.
Corresponding
increase occurs in
marriage (now
balanced).

Balanced nuclear
family. Similar
process will tend
to occur in ex-
tended family.

Bowen recounts that none of these methods were entirely satisfactory and that between 1962 and 1964, he developed techniques that he still uses. "In this format, I control the interchange. Each spouse talks directly to *me*" [(8); my italics]. Other techniques that Bowen mentions using, especially in early phases where anxiety is high, are focusing on process rather than content; taking distance; using humor; and communicating "I positions." The last is defined as the statement of one's own convictions and beliefs, and as the taking of action thereon without criticism of the beliefs of others and without becoming involved in emotional debate.

Interestingly, much as ontogeny recapitulates phylogeny, the course of Ackerman's approach to the family in our example recapitulates the sequence of stages in Bowen's account of his own development of an approach that worked.

Both had difficulty gaining entry. Both recognized the triangulation patterns but were unsuccessful in changing them directly. Both initially concentrated on intrapsychic content of the spouses and later switched to interpersonal content between them. Finally, both took a central position in the therapeutic system, focused on process, and took full responsibility for their own part of the process in relation to each of the other participants. Now the family began to improve.

Bowen puts it thus: " A basic principle in this theoretical therapeutic system is that the emotional problem between two people will resolve automatically if they remain in contact with a third person who can remain free of the emotional field between them, *while actively relating to each*" (9).

## The Key is for the Therapist to take Responsibility for Self

If the therapist takes full responsibility for self, *exactly the way he or she is*, he cannot *pretend*[4] to take responsibility for

[4]Pretending to take responsibility for another is usually manifested by trying to change the other. *Being* responsible for another is accepting that person exactly the way he or she is.

another and, most important here, none of the others can take responsibility for him; each has the opportunity to take responsibility for self in order to relate to him. Moreover, if two people are taking responsibility for self vis-à-vis a third in view of each other, they are simultaneously relating to each other as whole people. This is a balanced threesome and must occur, in my opinion, in all successful treatment situations.

A few more quotations may help make the point.

Again Bowen: "The more the therapist can clearly define himself in relation to the families, the easier it is for the family members to define themselves to each other" (9).

Listen to Bell: "The therapist demonstrates, often in response to tests by family members, that he or she will take certain stands." "The therapist will not take over family roles from individuals." "The therapist maximizes therapy power by limiting his or her behavior, a paradox made understandable by the pressures this exerts on the family to mobilize themselves." "The therapist keeps alert to the interaction taking place." "The therapist continues concentration on the involvement of family members." "The therapist is present both visibly and in action within the therapy situation and in the intervening periods between sessions." "The therapist continues to be taken into account because they know they must face the therapist at the next session" (10).

Witness Whitaker: "One of the most useful aspects of this kind of non-theoretical approach is the therapist's freedom to not demand or even push for progress." "The therapist should be able to reverse roles in such a way... that he allows himself to be coopted by the family system as its new scapegoat; *he can then prove that he can break his way out*" [my italics]. "He must develop the courage to be himself." "He must expand his own person." "He also exposes the fact that he cares more for himself that he does for them" (11).

Finally, Freud: "I cannot recommend... emphatically enough to take as a model the surgeon who puts aside all his own feelings, including that of human sympathy.... The affective impulse of greatest danger [to the success of treatment] will be the therapeutic ambition.... [Otherwise, the therapist] will find himself... helpless against certain... resistances *upon the struggle with which the cure primarily depends*" [(12); my italics].[5]

## Style and Becoming a Family Member

All these therapists "enter the family" to some degree. More accurately, the therapist forms a therapeutic system with one or more family members by becoming emotionally and/or cognitively significant to them. The degree of "significance" is measurable by the amount of time family members think of, experience emotions regarding, or talk about the therapist. In this special sense, it is my contention that the more poorly a family functions, the more "significant" a therapist must become to be effective. For instance, a family that can make decisions and take effective action is much more likely to accept, from a trusted authority, guidance that, if correctly prescribed, will help them to balance their own relationships. They will therefore need less to rely on the ripple effects of the process in the therapy system.

The family that functions poorly rarely has a member who can make independent movement that is large enough or sustained enough to create change in the family organization. The family is either too amorphous or too rigid. In my topography the amorphous family exhibits severe fusion in one or more relationships. Here, the therapist must, in my experience, become as significant as any member of the family. Then and only then do the therapist's personal moves engender family changes. By "moves" I mean increasing or decreasing interaction in any number of relationships; refusing the preferred over- or underfunctioning role (either by assuming the opposite

[5]It is interesting that the more recent Strachey translation changes the words to "depends on the interplay of forces in him," making it intrapsychic. The context of the sentence and the whole paper, however, is definitely interpersonal.

or simply taking responsibility for self); or both. Initially, the therapist, in Minuchin's terms, "accommodates" the family to the point of becoming "enmeshed" in the family and not extrudable by them. This, in my opinion, is what Whitaker is describing in the above quotations and why he has to "break out." In fact, as he mentions in the same paper, it is a good idea for a therapist working with such families to have a co-therapist or support system that can drag him out by his heels when necessary. Hill makes a similar observation about extremely impoverished families and certain concentration-camp victims (13). In such families, any change in organization almost necessarily involves crisis.

In the rigid family, one with well-entrenched patterns of triangulation, the therapist need not become as "significant," nor are the changes so dramatic. As Bowen describes, simply differentiating oneself while maintaining contact with the family members is enough to initiate and sustain the therapeutic process. One of the arts of therapy is knowing how far one can go and still maintain contact — that is, assessing the strength of one's relationship with the family.

In the successful psychoanalysis, the analysand is encouraged to attempt to fuse with the analyst while the analyst maintains himself with analytic detachment and persistent noncritical refusals to accept the roles proferred by the analysand. The analyst is always a significant other to the family, and family members regularly triangulate about this figure. Ideally, the analysand will eventually change his or her percepts and concepts of the analyst and come to react differently with family members.

Many therapists, of course, deal with families without becoming a significant other. They enter the family only to a minimal degree. In general, these therapists utilize "benign trickery" (Carlos Castaneda's aforementioned phrase) to remove a symptom or a "problem." Sometimes the trickery is deliberate and sometimes it is unintentional. Sometimes it results in an actual change in family process and sometimes not. When actual change occurs, the far-reaching effects are profound. Unfortunately, the family is pretty much on its own in handling the effects and may have losses along the way. In compensation, however, most families have a large armamentarium of natural healing techniques, and breaking up dysfunctional organization will often lead to well-functioning organization without further guidance. These points will be taken up in greater detail in the chapter on techniques. For now, suffice it to say that most of these methods are brief, and many of them are formularized to the extent that one therapist can be exchanged for another without much effect. In some cases of behavioral modification, for example, one can use written instructions effectively. Style, then, surely is not important to outcome here.

## What Style Is

Why then, do family therapists talk so much about what I would call style? On a superficial level, it is what hits us first when we watch a session. It is often what entertains us or "turns us off." It is what determines the degree to which we can identify or wish to identify with the therapist. On a slightly deeper level, it is what we as therapists struggle constantly to find as we strive to maintain our own differentiation in the endless stream of families who touch us; for the style that is our own is what we often identify as our "self."[6] Finally, because our conceptual tools have been meager, it is much easier to talk about style than to talk about process.

In terms of my constructs, therapists struggle with the same thing all humans struggle with — namely, the optimal interpersonal distance or degree of interaction for them. This is the point at which one can maintain direct, personal interaction with another; that is, the point at which one has neither to dramatize one's reactions (tend to fuse) nor to suppress one's reactions (tend to insulate). This point is different for different therapists, and different for different families. But the optimal

---

[6]*The* Self I assert to be more fundamental than thoughts, sensations, or emotions. Style is only a manner of presenting Self. Self is the awareness or level of consciousness that one can offer others and, as demonstrated by Bowen or Ackerman, transcends style.

points must be within reasonable range of each other for family and therapist to be usefully engaged. Some therapists operate best when they allow themselves to overreact up to the point where they are still capable of transcending their emotions and able to "pull out" — that is, decreasing the interaction without cutting off completely. Other therapists are more comfortable maintaining one position that allows them to keep in touch with the family without reacting at all. Bowen says, "If I am too close, I can get caught in the seriousness of the situation. If I am too distant, I am not effectively in contact with them. The 'right' point for me is one between seriousness and humor, when I can make either a serious or a humorous response" (14). Still others are at their best when constantly changing the pace of interaction — now very involved with the family, empathic and expressive of their own emotions; now remote or reflective.

This is the essence of style. It is determined largely by the patterns in the therapist's own family. This is a very complex matter, but to distill it for now, it can be said that the therapist who tended to be extruded from his family had to learn how to join in order to differentiate himself, whereas the therapist who tended to get "sucked in" as a youngster found the road to health by learning how to separate. (I use *join* to denote relatively intense interaction with balanced functioning, as opposed to fusion. I use *separate* to denote a balanced decrease in interaction without insulation.) I believe that those who function best by changing positions frequently are those who grew up with shifting triangles, but I do not have enough data on this point yet.

## The Importance of Style

Is style of any importance to therapy? Style determines the fit of family to therapist. Just as a 5-foot-tall man rarely "clicks" with a 6-foot-tall woman, so not every therapist is made for every family. On the simplest level, one shouldn't insist one can treat a French family if one doesn't know a word of French

—even though in all successful therapies the family must learn the therapist's language. More important, for the achievement of balance in the therapy system, one must first become part of the system and therefore must be able to speak the emotional language of the family. I know what Whitaker means when he says that "the only personal response to primary-process communication is primary process" (15). Whitaker, I am certain, can be with and evoke changes in families that other therapists could not tolerate — and vice-versa. (By *tolerate,* I mean be nondefensive to a point that one can establish a person-to-person relationship with each and every member. It is not necessary to actually do so, but one must be able to.) It is probable that many failures in family therapy are due to improper fit, and it behooves the therapist to have enough self-knowledge and enough courage to refer a family elsewhere when such is the case. I believe that there are impossible situations. I do not believe that there are impossible families.

Let me now expand the title of this chapter: Style is irrelevant to family therapy as a process or theory of behavior. It may be very important to the therapy of families.

# References

1. Wynne, Lyman C., personal communication.
2. Bowen, Murray, personal communication.
3. Ackerman, Nathan W., "The N Family," unpublished film (Ackerman Family Institute, n.d. [c. 1963]).
4. van den Blink, Arie J., audio tapes partially transcribed as "An Interview with the Lehrers," in van den Blink, *The Helping Response.* (Princeton, N.J.: Princeton Theological Seminary, 1972), 182-212.
5. Bowen, Murray, "Principles and Techniques of Multiple Family Therapy," in Guerin, Philip J. (ed.), *Family Therapy,* (New York: Gardner, 1976), 393-404.
6. Ibid., p. 402.
7. van den Blink, Arie J., transcription and notes on "An Interview with the Carpenters," in van den Blink, *The Helping Response,* 105-138.
8. Bowen, Murray, "Principles and Techniques of Multiple Family Therapy," in Guerin, *Family Therapy,* 388-404.

9. Bowen, Murray, "Theory in the Practice of Psychotherapy," in Guerin, *Family Therapy*, 42-89.

10. Bell, John Elderkin, "A Theoretical Framework for Family Group Therapy," in Guerin, *Family Therapy*, 129-143.

11. Whitaker, Carl, "The Hindrance of Theory in Clinical Work," in Guerin, *Family Therapy*, 154-164.

12. Freud, Sigmund, "Recommendations for Physicians on the Psychoanalytic Method of Therapy" translated under supervision of Joan Riviere (London: Hogarth Press, 1956), 327.

13. Hill, Rodman, "Treating the Black Family," unpublished videotape.

14. Bowen, Murray, "Principles and Techniques," in Guerin, *Family Therapy*, 397.

15. Whitaker, Carl, "The Hindrance of Theory," in Guerin, *Family Therapy*, 163.

**IX**

# THE RELEVANCE OF TECHNIQUE TO A THEORY OF FAMILY PROCESS

**t**echnique refers to "a body of methods... relating to a practical subject organized on scientific principles" (Webster's Third New International Dictionary). Thus, while both style and technique refer to a manner of doing, style has more to do with the personal characteristics of the doer, whereas technique presumably comes out of the knowledge that the doer has about the art or science in which he or she is engaged. Style captivates neophytes. More advanced students on the clinical firing line worship technique. Finally, after achieving a certain level of competence, one may come to the realization that having technique without a fundamental point of view from which to come is of little value. Indeed, technique comes out of one's point of view or out of how one holds one's observations — that is, out of one's theory.[1]

A useful theory must be able to include many techniques under its descriptive umbrella and account for successes and failures. In this chapter, I will examine examples of competent therapists using diverse techniques and see if the theory put forth in this book can be used to describe the way they operate. Because a detailed description of.these therapists' own working theories is beyond the scope of this book, readers who are not conversant with the examples used may find parts of this chapter unclear to them. My recommendation is to be content with the lack of clarity, get the general idea, and read the references if interest persists.

One value of a theory is that it helps those who already know the phenomena to talk with one another. Another value of a good theory is that it raises more questions than it answers. Still, it is reassuring when the constructs that we elaborate to order our own experience can also include the experience of others. (Some people like to call this "explaining.")


## Behavioral Modification

A number of years ago at a conference in Philadelphia, the therapist John Reid was explaining how he helped families with predelinquent youngsters by using behavioral modification techniques (1). First, he set up operational definitions of the bits of behavior he wished to extinguish (for example, stealing, lying, and cursing). Next, he designed a chart that depicted the number of undesired bits of behavior day by day, so that the family and he could track the behavior. Finally, after establishing a baseline, he instituted a token reward-and-punishment system that consisted of putting zeroes on the chart when the undesired behavior occurred and gold stars in the appropriate boxes when the behavior did not occur. Since the chart was displayed prominently in the home, the teenager

[1] I use theory to mean a set of fundamental principles within which there may be many theorems and concepts.

would see it and be affected by it. Sure enough, in the course of several weeks, the offensive behavior definitely decreased. The improvement rate of these generally refractory predelinquent boys was remarkable, but in accord with well-established behavioral principles.

Reid found that the mothers in these families also needed behavioral modification because their tendencies to rage at the youngsters would obscure the token-reward procedure. Accordingly, he taught them to take "time out" by using Jacobson's exercises[2] to relax and desensitize themselves to the youngsters' provocative stimuli. In addition, the mothers were instructed to leave the room when they noted their emotions about the youngster becoming intense. Perhaps for the same reasons, the fathers were given the task of setting up the chart at home and making the judgments about the behavior. They were instructed to be the final authority on what constituted stealing, lying, or whatever, and to pronounce verdict without allowing debate. The upshot was to decrease interaction between mother and adolescent and to increase interaction between father and adolescent, leading to more balance in the threesome (Figure 9.1a).

There are many other aspects of the above example that can be adequately described with our theory. First, the adoption of this plan called for agreement on the part of the parents, who, in many of these families, had difficulty agreeing and tended to triangulate around the adolescent. For these parents, communication was begun, and the barricading diminished. Second, the agreement required that the wife (who tended to be pseudoresponsible, either with son, husband, or both) delegate authority to the husband; and that the husband (who tended to be nonresponsible) assume new responsibility. Moreover, the husband had to take stands or "I positions," and doing so not only differentiated him, but also increased his importance to both wife and youngster. (These conclusions were drawn from anecdotal material given by the therapist as well as from a videotape that he presented.)

Finally, the therapist and the therapeutic system should

[2]Progressive skeletal muscle relaxation, sometimes coupled with self-induced visual and auditory relaxing images.

Figure 9.1

Father distant and barricaded from son. Mother pseudo-responsible and intensely involved with son.

Putting father in charge increases his involvement in pseudoresponsible way and deintensifies mother-son relationship.

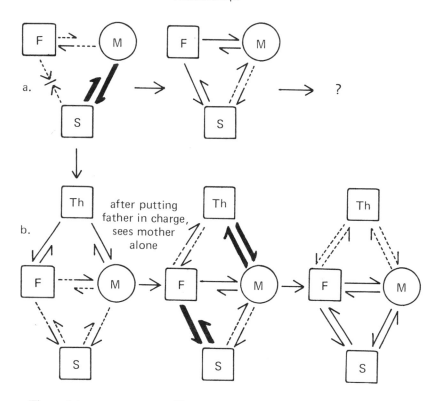

Therapist assumes pseudoresponsible role toward parents and son distances allowing father to break through with son albeit pseudo-responsibly.

Therapist shifts to mother and balances his relationships. Father intensifies his relationships and mother now able to balance with son.

As therapist disengages, son becomes actively related in balanced threesome.

not be overlooked. The therapist was very persuasive and took strong stands before asking the father to do likewise. He tended to relate more to the parents than to the adolescent. At one point, he saw the mother alone, supplanting the position of the adolescent. Later, he saw the whole family again and "reinforced" the parents' success. A good case could be made for the therapist's having become part of the triangulation process, balancing the threesome, assuming responsibility for self in all relationships, and then disengaging himself and allowing the adolescent to resume the vacated position in a more functional way (Figure 9.1b).

## *The Disadvantages of Restricting One's Point of View*

That this was done without the therapist's having thought of it in this way does not affect the process. It will, however, affect the way the therapist reports a success and the way others will understand the effort. It will also affect the data elicited if a follow-up study is made. One who is concerned with the whole family would be interested in a follow-up on the marital relationship. Many therapists would have been focused on the marriage during the course of therapy as well, even if the parents and therapist agreed not to work on it. Others might pay little attention to the marriage and neglect to help the parents with it, even if the parents were willing.

The danger of not having a whole-family point of view is that a therapist may unwittingly leave the client with more trouble after than before treatment. DiScipio, an accomplished behavioral therapist, relates the story of a man whose obsessive thoughts of other women were getting in the way of his marital relationship. He came to therapy concerned about his marriage. To relieve the symptom, a flooding technique was used that included the extensive recording of the thoughts in a journal. The thoughts faded away, and open conflict became intense as there became less to triangulate about. Unfortunately, the man handled this situation by allowing the journal to fall into his wife's hands, with disastrous results (2). It takes courage to report a poor result, and such a finding might not even be made by someone without a family orientation.

## Behavioral Modification and
## Degree of Involvement of Therapist

In Chapter VIII a distinction was drawn between those therapists who stay outside the family system or do not become a significant other and those who enter the family personally. These are two extremes of a continuous spectrum, one of which is typified by behavioral modification. In general, those who rely on giving explicit and more or less elaborate instructions to a family tend to become less significant personally. This does not mean that the therapist is less important, but rather that the family focuses more on the directives than on the person. Conversely, fewer explicit instructions are given by therapists who rely largely upon their personal relationship with members of the family and on their position in a therapeutic system.

As Haley points out, all therapists give directives, if only by a nod of the head. Although he is correct that directives "intensify the relationship with the therapist" (3), there is a difference between indicating "I am interested in what you are talking about" and saying "logically, you must do these things if you are to accomplish your aims." The former is a personal invitation. The latter is an opportunity to triangulate around the task, and the family generally grasps at it. What they talk about or think about is precisely not the therapist, but the task. This keeps the relationship between therapist and family members more distant and makes it easier to separate later on. It also makes it easier for therapist or family to drop out of the treatment system.

Moreover, if the family does not accomplish the task or if they cannot be motivated to succeed in other tasks, the therapist can have little impact. As Haley further states, if the therapist does not follow through on the task, the family will tend to drop it and not take other tasks seriously. I cannot agree with him, however, when he says that failure on the part of the therapist to follow through on a given task will make the therapist less important to the family. On the contrary, it may endear him to the family or result in resentment. Either would create more attachment on the part of the family to the person of the therapist. This, in turn, would make it more difficult to separate eventually, but it would also mean that if the therapist chose to get closer to or more distant from any member of the family, such "moves" would have greater effect.

## Behavioral Prescription and Reframing

John H. Weakland and others (4) at the Mental Research Institute in Palo Alto, California, view family problems as consisting "most basically of vicious cycles, involving a positive feedback loop between some undesired behavior and inappropriate efforts to get rid of it" (5). They rely, therefore, on "behavioral prescription and reframing the situation so as to make different problem-handling behavior seem logical and appropriate to the participants." In "The Z Case" (5), Weakland begins on the telephone, giving a distraught mother the directive to offer her divorced and remarried husband the opportunity to come with her to a counselor to talk about their truant son. The mother and son were intensely involved, and father had been criticizing mother's handling of son for four years. The father's reaction was to oppose the idea of treatment and take the son to live with him.

This major event illustrates the impact a faceless therapist may have on a family, especially when he gives instructions. Weakland considered this to be a mistake in that the family did not do what he suggested, but it may have been very helpful. It enabled mother and son to take a respite from each other for awhile. It put father in a more responsible position with respect to mother and son. It removed mother from between father and son (a position, said Weakland later, that the mother had been in). All in all, it was a balancing move, a move toward health. Such a move is drastic, of course, and rarely can be a final solution if there is a well-entrenched pattern of mother-son intensity and peripheral father. It has the special advantage, however, of giving father a chance to see what the firing-line is like, and it tempers blaming and criticism.

In this case, "quite a few months later," the woman again called to say the father was doing no better than she and that he was willing to come in. In this, the first session, Weakland describes himself as eliciting "behavioral information" and implies that he did not intervene in any way. I get the impression that he related much more intensely and supportively to mother than to father. He states from the beginning that he wanted to work with the mother alone, for instance, and in this session, he addressed the mother first, because "she had been the prime mover." A week later, the mother called again to cancel, saying (of her husband) that "he has always been leery of psychologists."

That Mrs. Z took the job of canceling Mr. Z's appointment fits with her pseudoresponsible middle position. Now Mr. and Mrs. Z are relating to the therapist as they had to their son. Something new is added. It is reported that Mr. Z is firmer with the son and that the son is behaving better. Weakland minimizes this report. To me, it makes perfect sense, the therapist has unwittingly taken the son's position in the family. They aren't functioning very well with him, but are doing better with the son (Figure 9.2a). People and families repeat their parentifying patterns of behavior with therapists, much as they do with certain children. Moreover, it is possible to be deeply involved with and reactive to a therapist without having laid eyes on the person. Many a spouse has reported to me a change in behavior (almost always on the part of the other) right after having made an initial appointment with me. It is surprising that many therapists who do not hesitate to call themselves manipulative and pride themselves on using almost any maneuver to change the family process seem oblivious to this enormous leverage.

Here, Weakland, worried that the family would not return, gives the mother the double message that she should come in anyway, but to think it over, take her time, and let him know. She did precisely that and called in "about a month" to say that the boy had been suspended from school and that the husband "now agreed to cooperate further, though somewhat reluctantly." This time Weakland suggested that the father not come in so as not "to draw on Mr. Z's limited store of cooperation" and agreed to see the boy at the mother's suggestion. (Weakland says "they" had it in mind that the boy should be seen, although he only spoke to the mother). Here he is assuming a pseudoresponsible attitude toward father, colluding with mother.

In this second session, Weakland spent a few minutes with mother and son and confirmed his impression that they engaged in cyclic debate and that the mother was very defensive. He then spent the rest of the time with the son. He told the boy he didn't *have* to go to school, that he shouldn't get A's and

Figure 9.2

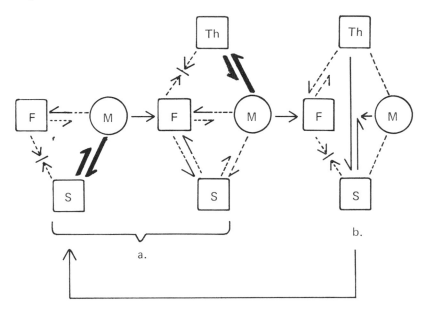

As mother and father focus on therapist, mother-son relationship becomes less intense and father-son relationship balances. (Father exerts natural authority and son accepts it.)

Therapist assumes pseudoresponsible attitude toward father and son. Barricading occurs between father and son again as mother disrupts therapist-son relationship and family returns to original pattern.

"confuse and rattle" his parents and teachers, and that he might get less hassling if he indulged in "apparent agreement" with his parents. Weakland calls this a "further intervention — the opposite of 'You've got big problems, and really need therapy.'" It is part of his rationale for seeing the boy, along with avoiding "redundant argument" and "helping my standing with Mrs. Z."

In any case, it is evident that Weakland had more contact with the boy than the mother. This is a radical shift for a therapist in a family where father and son don't get along and mother has to be in the middle. In the sparse description of the interview with mother and son, mother immediately cuts off son before he can answer a question by Weakland. Weakland's answer to this moments later is to exclude mother from the session. This results in Weakland supplanting mother's position (Figure 9.2b). Although Weakland excuses it, I would guess that mother's failure to call back for an appointment after this session was a reaction to this shift. After all, she had been very dutiful about telephone calls in the past.

"About a month later," mother calls once more, this time to say the father had "thrown up his hands," the boy was back with her, and things were worse than ever. As Weakland says, they had "been going around in circles." At this point, Weakland makes a strong pitch for seeing the mother alone and does so for two sessions. He is very accommodating. He relieves her guilt by acknowledging her mistakes without condemnation (he calls this reframing) and offers good guidelines in handling her son.

All his suggestions would tend to decrease interaction between mother and son. He agrees with her on everything and is careful to couch his advice in terms that are consistent with her beliefs. In a word, he maintains the nonresponsible position he was assigned initially. He perpetuates this at termination by telling the mother that she can call him when she wants. Toward the end of the last session, Weakland suggested to the mother that she tell her son that "his father was a difficult man." This was intended to get mother "out of the middle" or "out of an undue responsibility" for the father-son relationship, to "move her [mother] toward a realistically equal or one-up position vis-à-vis her ex-husband" and to "present Jacky [the son] with a realistic challenge to which he is likely to respond better than to 'Why don't you get along better with your father?'" He also makes a suggestion that "could really blow him [the father] out of the water" if he should "again get on her case" — namely, for mother to agree with father's accusation. Weakland states that mother's "own reaction" to accusations usually was, "Really, it's not all my fault,"; apparently, then, he is still thinking primarily in terms of mother's guilt. He offers no explicit rationale for getting mother "out of the middle" or challenging the son.

My own view, of course, is that all these tactics, if successful, would move the family toward a balanced threesome. They would tend to decrease interaction between mother and son and to increase it between father and son. They would tend to enhance mother's taking responsibility for herself rather than for others and would promote the possibility of breaking through the father-son barricade. Unfortunely, there is no further information on these matters, although Weakland did make a follow-up telephone call seven months later and found that "generally things were much better," even though mother still had to "bite back some of her old reactions." I would guess that Weakland's tendency to take the non-responsible position vis-à-vis mother and to remain barricaded with father makes it difficult for further improvement to occur.

A strong case can be made here, I think, for the importance of the form of therapeutic intervention, rather than the content. When Weakland responded to the mother, things got better. When he saw the boy alone, things got worse. When he concentrated on the mother again, things got better. The mother did carry out one or two of the actual suggestions made by Weakland, such as locking the door when the boy was out late, but she herself suggests that the difference was that she "backed off, not nagging so much," terms never used by her or Weakland before. Indeed, Weakland placed little emphasis on the amount of interaction between mother and son, either in his report or in his dicussions with the mother. Some of his statements (such as telling mother that she was the crucial one to evoke change in the boy) and almost all the directives could have been used to increase interaction if the mother desired.

That she actually decreased interaction, I attribute mainly to the therapist's role in the family process rather than to his words. One of the central notions of Weakland and his colleagues is that because positive feedback sustains process, reversing a circle or establishing a new one can have long-term, wide-ranging effects. I see no evidence for that in this case; rather, the woman seems to be hanging on to her small gain by keeping the therapist in mind. To quote Weakland, "she recalls some of the things I told her, and uses them at times, 'though I may feel I have a bleeding tongue.'" This is hardly a positive loop. It is apparent, however, that after seven months, the therapist is still of some importance to the woman; the second stage of Figure 9.2a may well be holding.

## The Tactical Therapies

Somewhere in the middle of the spectrum of those who become directly involved with the family personally and those who tend to avoid personal exchange are Minuchin and Haley. Each has been influenced by the other, although they developed from different frames of reference. Both are teachers. Both rely heavily on tactics. Both see the central importance of the therapist in the therapeutic system. Both theorize about family organization in spatial terms. Both limit their theorizing to descriptions that are immediately derived from or applicable to technique.

### Structural Family Therapy

The reader of Minuchin will easily recognize the similarities of his concepts of enmeshment and disengagement to the concepts called fusion and insulation in this book (6, 7). Minuchin does not generalize these concepts, however, nor does he talk about their reciprocity, although he does describe some families as alternately enmeshing and disengaging. Likewise, he does not appear to see triangulation as ubiquitous, but limits his discussion to specific examples of this process, such as detouring and coalition formation.

Minuchin uses a large variety of tactics, including the as-

signment of tasks, redefining a symptom, psychoanalytic interpretations, and gestalt imagery evocation. He is most famous,
though, for his dramatic use of the here and now in reenact-
ments of family behavioral sequences — taking sides with one
member against another, rearranging families physically, and
exhorting and compelling confrontations. Despite the vast difference in tactics as well as style, Minuchin's "restructuring"
(he has unfortunately borrowed the static term from the lin-
guists in lieu of the term *process*), turns out to be precisely the
same as that of the other successful therapists discussed here.
When two "subsystems" of a family, particularly parent and
child, are enmeshed (fused or engaged in relatively intense
interaction), he attempts to "establish clear boundaries" (separate, differentiate, or decrease interaction). When the boundaries are too rigid and the subsystems are disengaged (insulated
or engaged in relatively little interaction), he tries to "recon-
nect" them (join them or increase interaction). If the peripheral
father is weak, efforts are made to "join" him and "strengthen
his position" vis-à-vis the mother (increase responsibility of
father and balance the marital relationship) as well as to make
him more "central" in the family. His observations of family
process, his goals and strategies fit this general theory very
well. What about the therapeutic operations of the therapist
himself?

Minuchin is acutely aware of the dearth of attention paid
to the therapist's formal role in the system. In comparing the
writings of family therapists to those of individual therapists,
he states in his foreward to Papp's anthology of family therapy
case studies (8), "We have been repeating the same mistakes,
talking about the family or the therapeutic process as if the
therapeutic system has a black hole occupied by an invisible
therapist who is not affected by the feedback process, and
whose operations are not part of the system itself." Also, talking about the "group of prominent family therapists" represented in that anthology, he says "I assume that the therapeutic
operations presented... are, at formal levels, isomorphic, but
we do not yet have a generalized conceptual framework for
integrating their various approaches."

Minuchin's operations are indeed isomorphic to the operations described in this chapter. In the first place, he is always an important personage to the family. Not only does he exhibit a forceful character, but he also works in an institutional setting, where he is part of the management. (Many therapists use hospitalization, day-care centers and other treatment modalities at their diposal. At one level, these are parameters of treatment. At a more abstract level, they are all means of inducing the families, in their idiosyncratic ways, to focus more on the therapist's operations. The use of medication, for example, can become a central issue about which the therapist can differentiate himself and allow the family members to take positions of their own). Often, Minuchin is supervising another therapist behind a one-way screen and walks into a session unannounced, sometimes to make a few commments and leave.

All these operations (including the tactics mentioned above) tend to increase the family's triangulation around the therapist or his ideas. If matters are left at the idea level, which can be done only partially by the therapist's giving directives and then leaving the matter entirely in the hands of the family, the therapist can remain relatively outside the system. In practice, this is rarely done, because there is a need to talk about directives, and if the talking is with more than one member of a family, one is involved in family process willy-nilly.

The second part of my argument here, however, is that Minuchin often becomes part of the ongoing family process, even when he says he is restructuring it. For example, in a deprived, fatherless family, he often finds a helpless mother who relinquishes control to a "parental child." His tactic here, is to "block" the parental child's operations and "mother" the mother. Of course, he is exactly superseding the parental child's position in this maneuver. Or, to put it another way, he allows the family to triangulate around him, relieving the parental child of the burden (Figure 9.3). This becomes therapeutic if the therapist, unlike the parental child, can avoid taking over the mother's function but sustain her while she assumes more responsibility (balances the relationship). Thus

Minuchin will teach the mother to operate with the other children (increasing the interaction, breaking through the barricade, or both) and will encourage her to get a boyfriend, go to church, or whatever might be appropriate to ultimately replace the therapist in the system.

## Strategic Family Therapy

Because Haley either doesn't treat or only presents his supervisee's families, it is not possible to talk knowledgably of him as a therapist. But he does teach. Moreover, he tells us that "clinicians are learning to think in the unit of three and

Figure 9.3

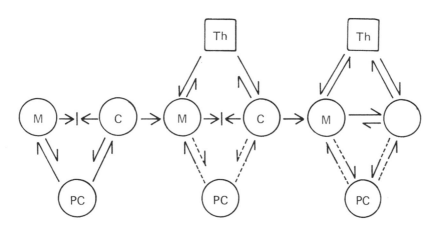

Parental child acts as manager for mother and sibling.

Therapist supersedes parental child.

Therapist balances his relationships and others in therapy system start to follow suit. Mother first breaks through barricade to become pseudo-responsible.

giving up the dyadic unit even when doing marriage therapy."
He also recognizes that the therapist "replaces the child with
the couple and thus stabilizes the dyad." He does not recognize
the threesome as a basic and viable way of functioning, however, for a moment later he states, "Then the problem becomes
one of how the therapist can exit without the couple unsta-
blizing and without bringing in the child again" (9).

Nevertheless, Haley's explicit concepts are very much in
line with my own, perhaps more than anyone else's. He is
obviously leery of theorizing, or he might have unified more
of his thinking. For example, in the case report titled "A Modern Little Hans" (10), Haley is quite explicit about using the
peripheral father to decrease the interaction between mother
and son by instructing father and son to get together in certain
ways. He never generalizes this principle to all triads, however,
and does not see that, as a supervisor standing behind a one-
way screen and never communicating with the family, but
only with the supervisee, he either tends to keep the supervisee
from getting too close to the family, (a good thing for neophytes,
generally), or triangulates him or her. This is enhanced by
Haley's retaining veto power over the student (11). To use
Haley's own terms, as he describes marital therapy (12), he is
forming a "constant coalition" to "destabilize" the therapeutic
system. He might claim that this is not a coalition as he defines
it, but rather an alliance. In my judgment, however, the crucial
element of a coalition is the need to exclude the third party.
Haley likes to confer outside the therapy room with his students, so that the family won't hear. Also, if one considers that
a supervisor is a generation ahead of students, Haley "crosses
generational lines" (13) with this practice (another destabiliz-
ing move), which must help the family to say goodbye faster,
in keeping with his emphasis on brevity.

It is difficult to say to what extent Haley's techniques would
take one inside the family, since he, like Minuchin, talks process mostly in connection with families, and tactics in connection with the therapist. He does say, however, that the
marital therapist is part of the process, like it or not: "Whatever
rules a couple is following, the therapist is part of the rules;"
moreover, he adds, "The therapeutic leverage comes in the

way the therapist changes that rule as it is used in relation to *him* (not by objectively commenting on it to the couple)" [(14); my italics]. This sounds amazingly like Bowen's "differentiating self" in the therapeutic system.

## Psychodynamic Family Therapy

At the other end of the spectrum is Whitaker, the exponent of personal involvement *par excellence*. In his "nontechnical or nontheoretical family psychotherapy," states Whitaker, "the therapy team establishes a pattern of caringness" and "models, with some member of the family, an I-thou relationship," much of which includes sharing "with the family the secret language that the therapist uses with himself." On the other hand, "once the therapist has been established, he denies all theory and forces the family to establish its own theoretical or systematic organizational way of living." "Once this fact has been settled and the family is clear that... the therapist does not know what is best for them, he becomes able to join the family as a consultant, to move into and to individuate from the family. By making it clear that his living is his own affair and must be handled in his own way, he moves out of the family" (15). This nontechnical technique, like the others, is of course a mix. Whitaker does give directives, sometimes explicit ones, as when he is instructing a mother to fight with her son (16), but he is still predominantly a nontactician working "inside" the family.

In a detailed report, Keith and Whitaker describe an example of this sort of treatment (16). Central in the treatment situation are Molly, a young woman trying to become divorced, her six-year-old twin boys, and Carl, the therapist. Carl has a "co"-therapist, Dave, who, however, is much less "co" than Carl and is relatively peripheral.

This mirrors the relationships of Molly and her parents, as the therapists observed after treatment was completed. They did not note, however, that it also mirrors the relationship between Molly and her husband and between Molly and the

Figure 9.4

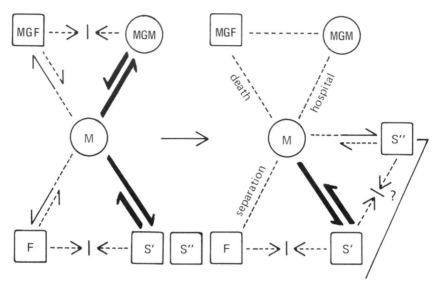

Nuclear family mirrors family
of origin.

Twin subsystem splits to replicate
pattern after marital separation.

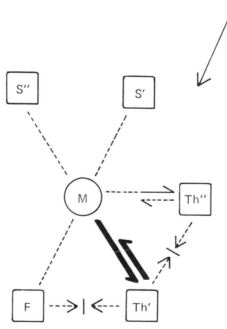

Therapists supplant twins and the
system replicates itself again.

twins as a unit during the marriage. After the separation, this constellation was in turn replaced by Molly and each twin as an individual (Figure 9.4). Molly's father is described as a "real person" but "distant;" her mother as "too intense, too closely involved." "Molly was locked into Carl in a way that was intense and confusing....Her relationship with Dave was much more distant, and frequently she directed angry and impatient feelings at him." Ed, the husband, is described as the one who "provided a reality orientation" in the marriage, much as the grandfather had been "the administrator." Likewise, grandfather is described as "cautious" and Ed as "halfhearted" — striving for closeness, but not making it.

The parents had been separated fifteen months at the onset of treatment, and the "twin boys, *especially Andy*, were into a grandiose trip. They had replaced the absent father and become a double husband to Molly" [my italics]. Despite this tendency of the authors to fuse the twins in their thinking, they tell us that "Andy was emerging as a covert scapegoat. He was having troubles in school, had started wetting the bed, and...had exhibited cruelty to animals....Tom [the other twin] was softer and an easily frightened child." One session is described in which Molly appears with Andy alone, "unable to handle him." "He had been dominating her at home."

It makes more sense to me to view the twins as replicating Molly's original family with her, and to view the co-therapy team as usurping this relationship. This is borne out by the fact that once co-therapy began (Carl saw parents and children alone for three sessions), "tussling with the children" began in earnest. "The fights with Tom and Andy would go on for entire interviews." "This play therapy with the children occupied much of the first four months." The authors view this as routine; "with omnipotent children," they state, "usually only a couple of visits pass by before their sense of omnipotence is extended to include the therapist." This apparently did not occur while Carl was seeing the family alone, however, even though "Carl and Molly developed an almost instant bilateral positive transference" and he "felt impotent about being able to handle the family in the face of the close lock-in with Molly." The rationale for calling in a co-therapist was to handle the children; my guess is that they became more challenging because the co-therapy team completed the original triangulation process and there was no role for the children. The therapists focused on the children rather than exclude them (Dave rejected Carl's original suggestion that he take the kids out into the playroom), and this decreased the intensity both between Carl and Molly and between Molly and the kids (Figure 9.5). As they say, "Our control provided her with some periods of happy distance from the kids." Note that the therapists provided to the boys both the pseudoresponsible role of mother and the barricaded role of father, while allowing the mother to continue her pseudoresponsible behavior with them. Thus the twins were usurped and maintained in relationship at the same time.

This is a beautiful example of the value of allowing one's

Figure 9.5

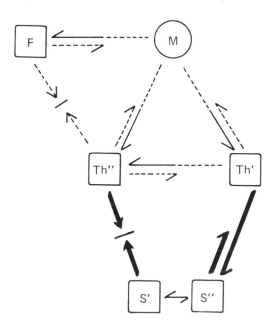

Therapists' intense interaction with
boys deintensifies mother-son relationship
and mother-therapist relationship.

moves to be determined by the system rather than worry about "being sucked in." These therapists were doing what the system seemed to demand, unmindful of the fact that for months they tried ineffectually to repeat the mother's efforts at control, and were actually doing a useful bit of rearranging by being in the middle between mother and sons. To the therapists, the intense reactions of the boys simply "wound down" in time, cured by the "almost developed...technique" of "overpowering the children and turning them back into little kids again."

From the larger view, I would say that this was made possible by the fortuitous establishment of a pseudo-extended family. Linda, the father's girl friend, became a regular attendee at sessions; she "had a strong transference to Molly" and "a secondary transference to Ed and Molly's marriage." This was possible because, although the therapists saw Linda and Molly as having "developmental similarities" because of "schizy and fragmented" mothers and "square" fathers, the two women occupied positions in their original families that were almost reciprocal. Molly had tended to be intensely involved with mother and a caretaker to her, while relatively distant from, but reactive to, her father.

The new combination of Linda, Ed and Molly was a similar but less intense and better-functioning replica. Linda tended to underfunction with respect to her father and to be distant and barricaded from her mother. She was therefore able to accept nurturing and control from Molly and stabilize rather than interfere with both the postmarital relationship and the mother-children relationship (Figure 9.6). It was noted by the therapists that "when it looked as though Ed and Molly might remarry...Linda was overwhelmed by the bond between them and started to withdraw." Also, although "the children steered clear of Linda," the "two women...were the best weekend parent set for the boys." Communication between Molly and Ed was clearer, and after termination, the intensity between Molly and Ed was still greater than between Ed and Linda, as indicated by a statement of Ed's reported by Napier: "There have been several occasions recently when I've talked with Molly and it's like talking to a friend that I'm not so entangled with. Just some anxiety or depression at the moment that it

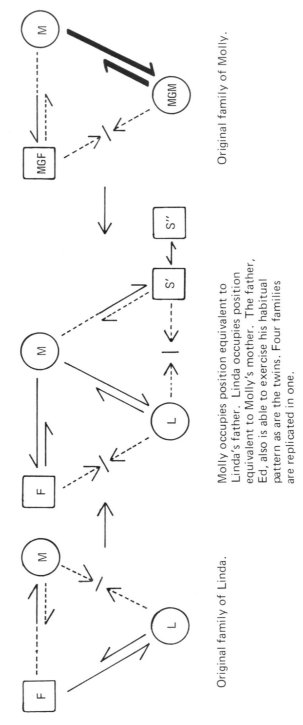

Figure 9.6

Original family of Linda.

Original family of Molly.

Molly occupies position equivalent to Linda's father. Linda occupies position equivalent to Molly's mother. The father, Ed, also is able to exercise his habitual pattern as are the twins. Four families are replicated in one.

was helpful to share with Molly, that it would be more difficult to share with Linda." Napier also says that "though Ed and Linda's relationship is more 'fun' than Ed and Molly's ever was, the major affective investment is between Ed and Molly (17). Note, however, that the relationship became much more balanced, with Molly and Ed "sharing," rather than Ed taking responsibility for Molly. Now the children can find a niche for themselves while Carl becomes more and more involved with Molly (Figure 9.7).

There is also a limited breakthrough with Ed as he goes through a "brief therapeutic psychosis" and even comes in alone, "confused and in a panic." He received support and felt "It was the first time anybody really cared about me, I think." This was just about the same time that Molly made a rapprochement with her mother. She had been ineffectual in trying to relate to this bizarre woman for years and had all but

Figure 9.7

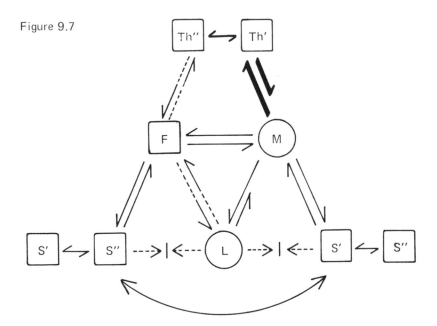

As therapists concentrate on parental pair, the central threesome begins to balance and the twins stabilize.

given up when grandmother was brought into therapy. (It is not clear how this came about and there are discrepancies between the therapists' account and Napier's follow-up.) Just as they had done with the children, the therapists intensely involved the grandmother and wrestled with her. At first they had a good time. Later, grandmother refused to come and "railed against that doctor who had brainwashed her." Nonetheless, Molly continued to see her mother with "coaching from Carl." She fought for her "autonomy," grandmother stopped fighting, and they were able to share some gifts and share the children. At the same time, Ed was making approaches to his mother and having "personal talks" in a way he never before experienced. Both grandmother relationships became more balanced, and the therapist was free to successfully terminate (Figure 9.8).

I cannot help but note once again the remarkable similarities between two such diverse therapists as Whitaker and Bowen. Although one focuses on children and the other excludes them, both supersede them in the therapeutic system. The rest of the family then includes the therapist in a triangulation process. Both participate to some degree. Both take responsibility for themselves and thus facilitate the family members' taking responsibility for themselves. In the therapy setting, they generally refuse to give explicit directives, but the behavior of the group is very much in line with the therapist's behavior. Both stress going back to the original family and both use the word *coaching* to describe their directives in this area. When a balanced relationship is established with a parent, there is a great improvement all around, with a concomitant decrease in intensity of the therapeutic relationship and subsequent termination.

These steps describe many successful family therapy endeavors. In fact, because the child or children who are superseded are also stand-ins for grandparents (see Chapter VI), many psychoanalyses could be described in these terms. Transference, from the point of view of relationships, could be called the supersedure of a parent or child by the analyst. Whenever I have been able to make specific inquiries about a successful psychoanalysis, I have found that both the analysand's percepts of and relationship with his or her original family had changed.

Figure 9.8

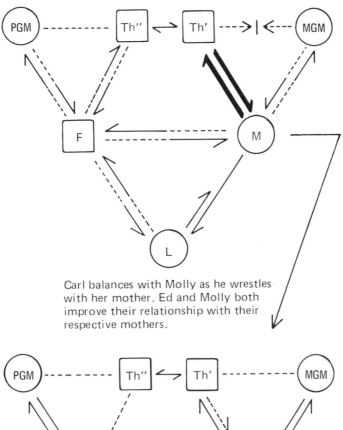

Carl balances with Molly as he wrestles with her mother. Ed and Molly both improve their relationship with their respective mothers.

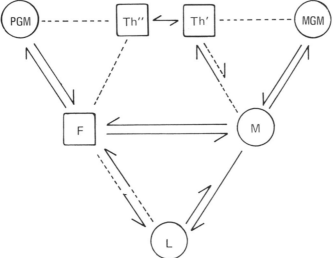

Solid relationships with both grand-mothers enable therapists to disen-gage with some residual activity.

# Conclusion

We have seen that a great variety of techniques of family therapy can be described in the same terms. This does not mean that each one does the same thing, but rather, that the fundamental process may be the same, even though the form can vary. Moreover, it is possible to find a common language that encompasses most techniques. If this language turns out to be an adequate description, then competent therapists can begin to usefully compare their different brands of therapy. Moreover, such a language would help in selecting and organizing data for meaningful outcome studies. It would be fascinating, for example, to determine what changes, if any, occurred in the extended families of those families that were helped successfully by a therapist who was not concerned with extended families. Likewise, it would be interesting to ask whether the changes in the nuclear family of an individual whose main treatment consisted of being coached in dealing with his original family turn out to be similar to the changes in a family whose therapist dealt exclusively with the problem presented.

One word of caution. Comparison does not mean competition. There is no best therapy, in my judgment. The distinction between style and technique is somewhat arbitrary and overlapping. Technique, like style, has to be suited to the therapist and the family. The purpose of comparisons, then, is not to end up with the technique, but rather to enable therapists to increase their versatility by expanding their armamentaria. Even more important, it might eventually enable us to match families with the therapist who is right for them.

Finally, this common language should not be used to teach beginners. Let my beginning readers be clear that all one can learn from a theory *alone* is the theory. Theoretical language is necessarily abstract and, to the neophyte, it is talking about a color never seen. At best, such learning is confusing; at worst, it is stultifying. The way to learn family therapy is to be with families in live supervision with a supervisor who can be a true consultant. A supervisor who meets this standard should be able to give adequate observations and relevant principles while insisting that the supervisee take responsibility for personal style and tactics. Such a supervisor should also meet the family and allow them to call on him or her if they wish. In other words, the supervisor should maintain a balanced relationship with the therapeutic system.

# References

1. Reid, John, "Behavior Therapy with Pre-delinquent Boys," paper presented at Frontiers of Psychotherapy: Behavior Therapy and Family Therapy (Philadelphia, 1973).

2. DiScipio, William, Chief Psychologist: Bronx Children's Psychiatric Center, personal communication.

3. Haley, Jay, *Problem Solving Therapy* (San Francisco: Jossey-Bass, 1976), 49.

4. Weakland, John H., Fisch, Richard, Watzlawick, Paul and Bodin, Arthur M., "Brief Therapy: Focused Problem Resolution," *Family Process*, 13 (1974), 141-168.

5. Weakland, John H., "OK — You've Been a Bad Mother," in Papp, Peggy (ed.), *Family Therapy Full Length Case Studies*, (New York: Gardner, 1977), 23-33.

6. Minuchin, S., Montalvo, B., Gurney, Jr., B.G., Rosman, B.L., and Schumer, F., *Families of the Slums: An Exploration of Their Structure and Treatment* (New York: Basic Books, 1967), 97, 105, 193-243.

7. Minuchin, Salvador, *Families and Family Therapy* (Cambridge: Harvard University Press, 1974), 53-56, 61.

8. Minuchin, Salvador, "Foreword," Papp (ed.), Case Studies, vii-viii.

9. Haley, *Problem Solving Therapy*, 154.

10. *Ibid.*, 222-268.

11. *Ibid.*, Chapter 7, 193.

12. *Ibid.*, 162-164.

13. *Ibid.*, 163.

14. *Ibid.*, 158.

15. Whitaker, Carl, "The Hindrance of Theory in Clinical Work" in Guerin, Philip J. (ed.), *Family Therapy* (New York: Gardner, 1976).

16. Whitaker, Carl, and Keith, David, "The Divorce Labyrinth," in Papp, Case Studies.

17. Napier, Augustus Y., "Follow-up to Divorce Labyrinth," in Papp, 133-142.

# CHAPTER X

# THE CANON OF
# FAMILY SYSTEMS

## Introduction

This chapter departs from the form of the previous chapters in order to fully communicate the formal and immutable quality of the laws of family process. Here are included definitions, rules, and canonical form. The canonical form is the most simple and clearest schema which can include all the vicissitudes of a process. Just as there is an endless variety of what we can do at the earth-space interface within the simple laws of gravity, so the richness of family life (and family therapy, I might add) is in no way limited by these canon. Rather, the rules, as always in life, provide us with the condition within which we can fully express ourselves.

# The Canon

**1. A family system is defined as people standing in constant interaction.**

**1.1.** *Standing* refers to maintaining a specified position or being in a particular state or situation.

**1.2.** That situation is constant interaction.

**1.3.** *Interaction* means mutual or reciprocal action or influence.

**1.3.1** An action is something done or effected.

**1.4.** *Constant* means continually occurring or recurring and is used here to distinguish between family systems and other people systems (such as work systems) that are occasional, that is, formed for a particular task or specified time.

**1.4.1.** This definition of family system would therefore include all groups committed to permanent relationships, such as communes and certain religious orders.

**1.5.** Another articulation of this definition is this: A family system consists of people maintaining a state of continually occurring reciprocal influence.

**1.6.** A more mathematical expression of this definition is that change of any measure of behavior of any person in a family system is a function of the same measure of behavior of all people in the family system. Conversely, a change of any measure of behavior of any person in a family system entails, first, change in all like measures of all other people in the family system, and second, change of the family system as a whole.

**1.7.** A corollary of this definition is that a family can only be known by the combination of its constitutive characteristics and its summative characteristics. That is, the relationship of its members must be known in addition to the characteristics of the members themselves. Moreover, some characteristics of the members themselves are different within the family than they are in isolation or outside the family.

**1.8.** Because the characteristics of a family system cannot be derived solely from the summation of the characteristics of its members, the characteristics of a family system appear as "new" or "emergent."

**2. Family process comprises all the family actions occurring during a given series of moments of time.**

**2.1.** An *action* has strength and direction and can be perceived visually, aurally, and kinesthetically.

**2.2.** An action can be directed at a person, at a relationship, or out of the system.

**2.2.1.** When directed at a relationship, an action may be followed by increased interaction in the relationship, in which case it is a *facilitating* action; or it may be followed by decreased interaction or cessation of interaction, in which case it is an *interruption*.

**2.2.2.** When an action is directed at a person and is followed by an action from that person toward the initiator of the first action, the two actions constitute an *interaction*.

**2.3.** Actions and interactions occur in *sequences*.

**2.4.** Sequences recurring two or more times constitute a *pattern*.

**2.5.** A pattern that is repeated more than most other patterns is a predominant pattern and is a criterion used to classify families on the basis of process.

**3. A threesome consists of any three entities of a family system, regardless of their patterns of relating.**

**3.1.** An entity is most often a person but may consist of two or more people that relate as a unit to other entities in a threesome.

**3.1.1.** Such multiperson entities can be termed subgroups.

**3.2.** Any family system can be viewed as a finite number of threesomes, each with its own patterns of relationship.

**3.2.1.** A three member family has one threesome, a four-member family has four threesomes, a five-member family has ten threesomes, and so on.

**3.3.** Any entity of a threesome may be said to "couple" the other two and its state is a function of the state of the other two. The converse is also true: *The relation of any two entities of a threesome is conditional on the state of the third.* (For example, whether a mother interrupts, remains silent, or speaks for father or child will have profound implications for the relationship of father and child.)

**3.4.** *The sum of the quantities of interaction of the three relationships of a threesome tends to remain constant.*

**3.4.1.** If A decreases interaction with B and C, then the interaction between B and C increases proportionately.

**3.4.2.** If A increases interaction with B or C, then the interaction between B and C must decrease. (For example, if a father increases interaction with a mother or child or both, the intensity of the mother-child relationship will decrease.)

**3.5.** A threesome is to be distinguished from what is sometimes called a "triangle," namely, three entities engaging in the process of triangulation (see section 7).

## 4. The health or well-being of a family can be measured by the proportion of balanced threesomes.

**4.1.** In a balanced threesome, *all three relationships exhibit approximately the same amount of personal interaction.*

**4.1.1.** Personal interaction is defined as interaction that conveys affect or belief regarding oneself or the relationship in such a way that the communication is received and returned in kind.

**4.2.** In a balanced threesome, *all three relationships are balanced with respect to responsibility.* Each person (or subgroup) assumes total responsibility for his or her behavior toward the others and accepts the assumption of total responsibility by the others for their behavior. The assumption of responsibility in no way hinges on the attitude or actions of anyone else, and therefore, it involves in each person a fundamental willingness to be responsible for the whole relationship. Once one person in a relationship adopts this attitude, there is no *requirement* for the other to be responsible and it is therefore easier for the other to assume responsibility.

**4.2.1.** Responsibility is being at cause in the matter. It is a point of view that has nothing to do with burden, fault, sacrifice, or guilt; in fact, guilt is an avoidance of responsibility.

**4.2.2.** The assumption of responsibility does not imply a knowledge of how one is at cause nor even the existence of a mechanism of cause; nor does it incur an obligation to do anything. It is the creation of a context out of which flows a willingness to do what is feasible and useful.

**4.2.3.** Once one acknowledges full responsibility for self as individual there is no limit to the area one may take on. One can assume responsibility at the level of relationship, family, clan, and so on. There is a major distinction, however, between assuming responsibility for self as individual *within* the family, and assuming responsibility for self *as* family.

**4.2.4.** Any person or all people in a system may assume total responsibility for the system in which one operates, however large or complex one considers the system to be.

**4.2.5.** If one relationship remains balanced in a threesome, the other two will become balanced.

**4.3.** If one threesome remains balanced in a family, the other threesomes will balance.

## 5. Other types of relationships are pseudoresponsible-nonresponsible, fused, barricaded, and insulated.

**5.1.** A *pseudoresponsible-nonresponsible* (or simply pseudoresponsible) relationship is one in which one person insists upon taking care of another whether caretaking is needed or not. In this sense, the caretaking person is actually under-responsive to the other. Moreover, whatever the caretaker does is viewed as an obligation often imposed by the other, so that the caretaker takes no true responsibility. The nonresponsible person can be helpless, indifferent, or objecting. He or she is often highly reactive and exquisitely sensitive to every move of the pseudoresponsible person, and in this sense is over-responsive.

**5.1.1.** People in a pseudoresponsible relationship may exchange roles from time to time.

**5.1.2.** Many pseudoresponsible relationships are marked by so much reactivity that it is difficult to distinguish one role from the other.

**5.2.** A *fused* relationship is a pseudoresponsible relationship carried to extreme. The two people are so locked into the pattern of the first person operating only for the second person and the second responding only to the first that they behave as a single individual.

**5.2.1.** One of a fused pair generally relates to the environment, but only about the needs of the pair, whereas the other relates only to the first.

**5.2.2.** A fused relationship may consist of more than two people.

**5.3.** A *barricaded* relationship is one in which communications are incomplete. The individuals either fail to insure that they communicate in such a way that their message will be received, or they do not listen attentively or, more often, they do neither.

**5.3.1.** Persons in a barricaded relationship may take responsibility for themselves as individuals but do not take responsibility for the relationship.

**5.3.2.** Persons in a barricaded relationship tend to behave as peers with respect to dominance and competency. (Spouses of similar sibling order frequently barricade.)

**5.3.3.** Barricading can take the form of open warfare, silence, or simply a continuous focusing on a third person, group, or thing.

**5.4.** An *insulated* relationship is so sparse with regard to interaction as to be a nonrelationship for practical purposes.

**5.4.1.** An insulated relationship is more likely to occur between peerlike individuals than in dominant-subordinate pairs, but insulated relationships are not necessarily limited to peerlike pairs.

**5.4.2.** An insulated relationship is incomplete for both parties, as manifested by easily evoked intense thoughts and emotions about the other.

**5.4.3.** An insulated relationship is kept so quite forcefully by the pair, who offer great resistance to any attempt to bring them together.

**6. Fusion and insulation are twin processes that occur always and only together in the same system. More accurately, they are the end points of the general system processes known respectively as progressive centralization and progressive differentiation.**

**6.1.** The actual occurrence of fusion and insulation is equivalent to the demise of the family. Near-fusion and near-insulation or frequent intermittent fusion and insulation can be considered a predominant pattern for clinical purposes.

**6.2.** The terms *fusion* and *insulation* are used in this canon only in the interpersonal sense.

**6.2.1.** Fusion can be seen as the end result of a progressively more intense and imbalanced pseudoresponsible relationship.

**6.2.2.** Insulation can be the end result of a progressively less intense barricaded or pseudoresponsible relationship.

**6.2.3.** An example of fusion and insulation is a symbiotic mother and child with a very peripheral father.

**6.2.4.** Fusion and insulation are intrasystemic states and not simple attributes of individuals. (For example, a man who is insulated from his family is not necessarily insulated from his work system.)

**7. Triangulation is the process in which one individual or subgroup stands in relation to two other entities in such a way as to be the focus of that relationship. The third member may be an intermediary or may be shut out.**

**7.1.** The shut-out third or intermediary is always in a pseudoresponsible relationship with the other two entities. The relationship of the other two is barricaded.

**7.2.** The intermediary or shut-out third serves the dual function of being a bridge as well as a barrier for the other two members of the threesome.

**7.3.** Triangulation may ocur in any threesome. The barricade may be between any two members or subgroups, and it may shift around.

**7.4.** Triangulation is universal and occurs in all families at times.

**7.5.** Triangulation may represent a shift toward balance if it occurs in a family previously characterized by fusion and insulation.

**7.6.** Triangulation occurs in three general patterns.

**7.6.1** *Focused triangulation* or triangulation with a shut-out member: The third member is often ignored. Interaction is much more frequent between the barricaded pair than in the other two relationships.

**7.6.1.1.** The third member is nonresponsible and may be almost inoperative.

**7.6.1.2.** The third member is pseudoresponsible as in the instance of a remote judge or dictatorial parent.

**7.6.2** Triangulation with an *intermediary*: The barricaded relationship exhibits little interaction compared with the other two relationships.

**7.6.2.1.** The intermediary is a message carrier or switch-board and is nonresponsible.

**7.6.2.2.** The intermediary is a manager and is pseudoresponsible.

**7.6.3.** *Shifting triangles* is that pattern in which the barricade shifts from one relationship to another from moment to moment. There is intense open conflict, with interruption after interruption. All are pseudoresponsible at times.

**8. On the basis of process, families can be classified into three general types.**

**8.1.** *Balanced*

**8.2.** *Fused and insulated*

**8.2.1.** Spouse-spouse or sibling-sibling fusion (*folie-à-deux*).

**8.2.2.** Parent-child fusion (symbiosis).

**8.2.3.** Amorphous family (more than two people fused).

**8.3.** *Triangulation predominant*

**8.3.1.** The barricaded relationship is intense and third member is nonresponsible (focused member or shut-out member).

**8.3.2.** The barricaded relationship is intense and third member is pseudoresponsible (distant judge or authority).

**8.3.3.** The barricaded relationship is meager in interaction and third member is pseudoresponsible (manager or referee).

**8.3.4.** The barricaded relationship is meager in interaction and third member nonresponsible (child message-carrier or switchboard).

**8.3.5.** Barricaded relationship shifts from pair to pair.

**9. Strategy of intervention (follows directly from classification).**

**9.1.** Balanced: No intervention.

**9.2.** Fused and insulated: facilitate interaction of insulated member with either or both of the others. Encourage all members to triangulate.

**9.3.** Triangulation predominant: facilitate completion of communications between barricaded pair; or interdict pseudoresponsible member(s) from doing for nonresponsible member(s); or support nonresponsible member in doing for self; or use any combination of these. Always facilitate interaction where it is sparse; dampen it where profuse. For shifting triangles, stop the action.

**10. Intergenerational laws are similar to those of the nuclear family.**

**10.1.** The tendency for quantity of interaction to remain constant holds up from generation to generation. Increasing interaction with one's family of origin will decrease interaction with one's nuclear family and vice-versa. (Strategies based on this law can be used to "detoxify" a nuclear or extended-family relationship.)

**10.2.** All the patterns of interaction remain operative in generation after generation of nuclear families, even when the interaction is very sparse. A parent will soon engage in the patterns of his childhood if placed in proximity with his or her parents.

**10.3.** An individual will tend to engage in the same type of relationships with his or her family of adulthood as in the family of origin. Hence, the threesome patterns of relationships will tend to replicate themselves generation after generation.

**10.3.1.** Examples of intergenerational transmission of relationship patterns include the following: A child who was a mediator between parents will, as an adult, tend to get between spouse and child. A boy who was barricaded with father and nonresponsible with mother might, as an adult, tend to be nonresponsible with his wife and barricaded with his son.

**10.3.2.** Fusion begets fusion, insulation begets insulation, and barricade begets barricade.

**10.3.3.** A pseudoresponsible parent will have a nonresponsible child and so on.

**10.3.4.** A child tends to have the same ways of relating as its grandparent.

**10.3.5** From generation to generation, relationships that are highly interactive tend to be reciprocal with regard to responsibility and dominance. Relationships that have little interaction tend to be symmetrical and peerlike.

**10.4.** Balancing one's relationships with one's original family tends to balance *all* one's relationships. Balancing one's relationships in one's family of adulthood will help to balance one's relationships in the family of origin.

# AFTERWORD

## About Well-Being

Having set down the rules of family process more or less, I will now say that the temptation to learn these rules thoroughly in order to develop a technique that will make families well is a waste of time. If that be your goal, nothing I have said in this book is worth remembering. One can assist families to accelerate if that family is already changing, but to be well is another matter. In fact, "doing therapy" is often a strong message to an individual, family, or organization that something is wrong. If that is one's fundamental point of view, all that can be done is to work toward getting better — to make changes, yes, to be *well*, no. Technique will not create well-being.

Moreover, the mere transfer of information cannot communicate that which one needs to know to master therapy. Nor can such knowledge be acquired experientially. If I were the most talented poet I could not evoke that which I now want my reader to grasp. I want my reader to grasp the vision that he or she is able to create a context of well-being and convey it to a family in such a way that the family members are enabled to create the context of well-being themselves, out of which they will experience themselves as well, and will begin to take the unique paths which will lead to health for this family; which, in turn, will ultimately change the circumstances of the family, including the way the members feel, think, and communicate. I call this the transsubstantiation[1] of a family and, just as some readers will make this leap with me, some families will do it and some won't. Families *become* well only after they apprehend that they *are* well, whole, complete, and perfect.

Much of what I've just said is not understandable. It needs to be prehended in a different realm of knowing than the one in which we generally operate when reading a book of this sort. We need to get beyond the conceptual realm. Neither can the poet, marvel that he is, do it for us. The artist's way of knowing can move us to great heights and depths and yet he is powerless here. That of which I now speak is not an experience, is not to be taken in by experiencing, is not a process to go through. It is that out of which experience flows. It is that out of which, according to Wittgenstein, we cannot speak. We can only use propositions "as steps — to climb up beyond them" (1).

I hesitate to name the realm I am talking about because it will immediately be conceptualized into a thing by any mind that reads it. I must therefore tell you that the name of it is not it. Nor is it explainable. I can only point to it and you, dear reader, must *see* it. And your *seeing* it must be a creative act, an existential act of courage. You must actually call it forth for your Self. You must generate this realm of knowing out of nothing. Some will see this; some will not. I am not insulting anyone's intelligence. The leap I am talking about has nothing to with "smarts." It has to do with the courage to *be*, to just *be*. What it takes is the willingness to stand entirely on one's own, to give up one's beliefs and one's story. If one is willing to live in this realm, I assert that one can *be* well, regardless of one's circumstances, including one's body, one's thoughts, and one's feelings.

[1]Transformation is the word in vogue, but I want to indicate a new essence rather than a new form.

I am not invalidating thoughts and feelings. I am not deny-
ing the circumstances people live in or the importance of
body states. I simply say that well-being lives in another realm
and that the web of interpretation we spin around our circumstances, which is so real to us, constrains us and also
*maintains* the circumstances. Einstein said, "Everyone sits in
a prison of his own ideas; he must burst it open... and so try
to test his ideas on reality" (2). The time has come for family
therapists to break out.
see it? I don't know how. I'm not even sure what. But others
have given witness that such *seeing* exists. Pater says, "For
such vision, if received with due attitude on (one's) part, (is),
in reality, the *being* something...." [(3) my italics].

Wittgenstein says, "My propositions serve as elucidations
in the following way: anyone who understands me eventually
recognizes them as nonsensical, when he has used them — as
steps — to climb up beyond them. (He must, so to speak, throw
away the ladder after he has climbed up it.)" (1).

So now we go up the ladder. There has been much pas-
sionate and beautiful argument about the "new epistemology"
in our field.[2] Among all the considerations, it seems to me,
there are two major muddles. One is that we confuse the rules
of thinking for the ways of knowing. Two is that we try to
improve on that way of knowing called thinking about it by
thinking about it some more. When that doesn't work, we try
to think about it better. And when that doesn't work, we try to
think about it differently. One example is the attempt to find
a mechanism for discontinuous change, not noticing that a
mechanism *is* a continuous change (4). One may as well seek
the mechanism of death or the mechanism of coming to life.
A more useful question would be, "What is the realm of knowing without time? And how can one communicate in that
realm?" I believe that the time has come in our field to transcend mere thinking about it. It is also time to recognize the
insufficiency of experience as a basis for knowing.

[2]The process is probably more valuable than the content. The polarization
acknowledges a division present in our field twenty years ago and, for
me, heralds the advent of the family therapy movement getting rid of this
"Us or Them" stuff.

Einstein said, "I believe in intuition and inspiration.... At times I feel certain I am right while not knowing the reason.... Imagination is more important than knowledge. For knowledge is limited whereas imagination embraces the entire world, stimulating progress, giving birth to evolution" (5).

Whatever Einstein means by intuition or imagination I take to be the same as that domain which Wittgenstein says "we must pass over in silence"(1), the same as that referred to by Pater as *seeing* — Carlos Castaneda has Don Juan using the same word (6) — by Werner Erhard as calling forth or creating context (7) and by Buckminster Fuller as generalized principles (8).

If one gets on a bicycle and peddles and falls off and gets up again and peddles and falls off and keeps at it long enough, most people will eventually be able to ride the bicycle. The question arises: Does this person now *know* how to ride a bicycle? The answer is no, if by knowing one means the ability to conceptualize and explain the riding of the bicycle. The answer is yes, if by knowing one means being able to ride the bicycle. Clearly, then, there are at least two realms of knowing. The first is the conceptual realm in which there is thinking, understanding, explanation, and all memory. This realm serves us well when doing brain surgery or trying to find our way home at the end of the day. The second is the realm of experience, an entirely different realm which is not at all an equivalent to or substitute for the conceptual realm. No amount of explanation or description of a painting, of a symphony, or of jumping out of an airplane, can take the place of the actual experience. Nor does an experience blueprint itself so that it can be duplicated or modified by others.

Among the properties of experience is that it only occurs in moments of now, that there is nothing one can do with it except experience it (it cannot be changed) and that it disappears immediately upon experiencing it. The realm of experience is related to the realm of concept in that experience is remembered and memory may be said to reside in the realm of concept. This is a double-edged sword, for although it enables the traveler to go back the way he came, the trip is now largely dominated by the memory of the original journey.

Moreover, one will tend to re-experience the original *even when the circumstances have substantially changed.* And this new experience immediately devolves into memory which, in turn, dominates the next experience which, in turn, reinforces the memory; and so we live in a self-reinforcing loop.

Most of us are commuters on the road of life who never notice that the scenery changes, who never take delight in new verdure nor are pained by its withering. We know when major events occur, of course, that we are supposed to feel sad or gay, and we live our lives consistent with that concept, but rarely do we experience fully what there is to experience. In fact, we do not distinguish between our experience and our concepts. We think that when we say "I love you" that that is the same as the experience of "I love you." How many of us are rapturous when we say to our loved one "I love you" the way we were when we first said it? Rapture, ecstasy, the thrill of being deeply moved: these are the experiences of "I love you." We are not, for the most part, experiencing "I love you" when we say "I love you." What we mean is, "I have experienced loving you and I live in congruence with that memory." And we don't even know that we are doing that. What's more, we don't want to know! It is sad to realize that one is not experiencing what one thinks one is experiencing and who wants more sadness?

We go on, then, not making the distinction between the realm of experience and the realm of concept and are trapped in the loop. We do not experience Jane or Jim or Pete or Susie. We experience female or black or elderly or kid. We do not meet people authentically because we are stuck in our concept-dominated-experience — experience-reinforced-concept — concept-dominated-experience cycles. And we don't know this because we failed to make the distinction between our experience and our thoughts and we can't make the distinction because we don't want to know and we don't want to know because it is painful and because it is awesome and fearful to take on responsibility for one's own experience.

When one actually does break out of the vicious circle, instead of taking credit for it and looking for the source within, we attribute the breakthrough to the circumstances and climb right back into the loop. We are deeply moved by a sunset viewed with a loved one in the Caribbean, and we go back home filled with the resolve to return one day to re-experience the joy. And we do just that. We even find the same restaurant with the same checkered table cloth and perhaps even the same waiter. But it is never the same. It is never the same because experience does not come out of the circumstances. Experience comes out of our Selves.

The poet communicates in the realm of experience not by the transfer of ideas but by the evocation of images to which we are open by *actively listening and looking*. The poet puts nothing into us. The poetry is in the listener and it is the poet's great talent to provide the listener with the tools to create the experience. But the poet uses only the circumstances that are available to the rest of us, nothing more. What, then, is the poet doing with *his* circumstances that the rest of us fail to do with ours? What does he or she do with his world, his sites, his people, his thoughts, his feelings, his body that we, for the most part, do not do?

The poet brings into being from the flat canvas of life a sharp relief. He creates River out of rivers, Time out of times, and Love out of loves. He is a connoisseur of life who can communicate in such a way that we, too, can *see* the Wine in wines. In turn, each wine is a new wine and ultimately we discriminate more and more clearly one from the other.

"Representation is a compromise with chaos whether visual, verbal, or musical. The compromise prolonged becomes a convention" (9). Conventions or ideals, as Berenson makes clear, are canonical forms which allow us to share the universe with others. This communication enables us to appreciate by differences from the ideal the many elements of our everyday experience. "Most conventions are concerned with the recognition of objects we want to approach or avoid, but some are representational" (10) or artistic. Thus, the process of inventing the wheel and inventing the nude is essentially the same. Although thousands of years may go into the refining and manipulating and keeping alive the convention, it is actually created in an instant by one being who called it forth, who languaged it. This existential act of courage, this generating of an Idea, this calling forth a Context belongs to another realm of knowing. It may be called the realm of Context or Creation or Calling Forth or simply Being. This realm is absolute; it is the only realm where certainty exists. It is full, unbounded, timeless, and complete. And it is only brought forth by an individual human being as a courageous act of creation. And like any creation it can only be brought out of nothing. This is the essence of *being* human: Nothing, out of which everything can be generated.

I say anyone can generate context if one is willing to be the cause of one's experience. And if one is willing to communicate the generation of context fully, one can be a powerful family therapist. There is no power, however, in explanation. Critics can explain Toscanini till the cows come home; they can never empower an orchestra. Sports journalists are not coaches and family theoreticians are not necessarily great family therapists. The former communicate by transfer of information in the realm of concept and the latter communicate by generating context and creating the opportunity for the *other* to generate context. This is what great teachers do when they "get the most" out of their students. This is what great therapists do when they enable a family to move to a higher level of functioning. And every therapist of some reasonable experience has been great at times. By contrast, explaining the ways of great therapists never replicated them.

When one generates the context of well-being with a family it gives the family the opportunity to *see* themselves as well; that is, to create for themselves the context of well-being out of which they will do the things that well families do and eventually will have the things that well families have. And when one is generating context as a therapist, one will do what works and what one does will work. One is able to be with the family and experience it fully as it truly is rather than as some poor reflection of one's theory which is but the memory of families past.

And so it is with the theory in this book. I have kept my theory as general and abstract as possible so that the student cannot simply sling it on his back like a bag of tricks and slavishly avoid using his own creativity. Does that mean we should throw out theory altogether? Not at all. We could not begin to communicate with experienced family therapists without theory, let alone interest students in the field. Besides, we are so constructed that we cannot help but theorize and to pretend not to is a useless waste of energy. What there is to do is to allow ourselves to theorize and include the domain of concept in the domain of experience by experiencing ourselves theorizing. We cannot be dominated by that which we cause. If we are willing to be the cause of our own experience we can generate our Selves as the context of our experience and *include* the domain of experience in the domain of context. We then operate in all the domains of knowing simultaneously and powerfully. We are the cause of our own experience and we now cause ourselves causing our experience so we can cause it at will.

What does this mean to the family therapist? It means that the opportunity is there for us to take it all on, one hundred per cent. We can establish the context of every therapeutic situation and cause the experience and the outcome. (I did not say manipulate the outcome.) This enables our families to take on one hundred per cent of the responsibility too, if they choose to do so. In fact, it is the only way they can take it on, for no one can be *made* to take responsibility. The opportunity, then, is not merely for the family to change, to operate in a different style or do different things, but to transsubstantiate itself and reach a whole new level of functioning. The actual therapy may look the same, but the point of view from which therapist and family comes is now of a different order and the outcome may be extraordinary. A dramatic shift takes place which is life enhancing and unexplainable. All experienced family therapists have had this kind of experience. The trouble is that they then explain the miracle by examining the circumstances (the current events, the setting, the techniques, even their own behavior) and, in attempting to reestablish those circumstances, never again produce the same results.

Explanations are a copout here. It is you yourself who created the miracle if you're willing to see. A master therapist is willing to cause the results whatever the outcome. He or she is willing to have it be exactly the way it is and not be exactly the way it is not. Families are not resisting or cooperating or good or bad. They are simply doing what they are doing, and whatever they are not doing is now simply a possibility which may show up. The master therapist *sees* the family in this way and shares the vision and is willing to cause Self causing the vision.

I say this power is available to everyone. It takes courage. It takes the willingness to "burst open...the prison of (one's) own ideas" (2) and stand nakedly on nothing. If this be your bent, you may start by simply allowing yourself to be the way you are as a therapist. If you are emulating a master, you are being your Self and if you are trying not to emulate a master you are being your Self. Take *full* responsibility for the outcome whatever it is. Your families will appreciate you and you may notice yourself creating a context of well-being for them.

## Beyond Family

And after family, what? It has been a most natural step for me to become interested in the work system. First, many of my families have family businesses which are deeply affected by and, in turn, affect family relationships. Second, my many students, I have found, often have less difficulty doing family therapy than they have dealing with the facilities in which they do family therapy.

By examining the work systems of students and members of families in therapy, two principles emerged after a rather short time and were refined over a period of one to two years: 1) Every individual tends to recreate his or her major family patterns in any small group and is more or less successful at it in time (this includes a therapist in a therapy group) and 2) Every small group system tends to have its content reproduced by other groups exposed to it by observation, by communication, or by having mutual members. The second principle tends to be more obvious, to be more transient, to manifest itself more concretely and to occur within the context of the first principle. Thus, the dominant conceptual themes, the experienced emotions and the degree of enthusiasm appear to be reciprocally affected by closely related family groups, by contiguous work and family groups, and by communicating work departments. If a supervisor-supervisee relationship tended to be harping and critical, so would the therapy system and so would the family system and *so would the seminar in which the examination of the other systems took place!* At the same time, the patterns of relating in the therapy system, in the work system and in the training system remained those of the family of origin of the particular student therapist. How neatly this dovetailed with the patterns of the family, the supervisor and colleagues is beyond the scope of this discussion.

In any case, these two principles proved to be very powerful and enabled one to become much more effective at work and with families. Often, after seeing a student with his supervisor and members of his supervisory group or seeing a supervisor with the supervisor's superior and peers, dramatic shifts would take place in the therapy system. All this was very exciting and made me think that mastery of the level of clan or organization was at hand. I found, however, that the transition from a grasp of family to a grasp of clan or organization was a much greater jump than the shift from individual to family. What I had been doing was becoming increasingly more effective with families and small groups by means of treating families in the context of their clans, much as many of the early family therapists actually treated individuals in the context of their families.

Another partial success was the discovery that the principles of triangulation could be applied to the relationships among small groups. For example, in working with the mobile treatment teams of a family-oriented treatment service I found that they were often the mediators of a barricaded relationship between the families of inpatients and the ward personnel. Once the mobile team family therapists stopped being pseudoresponsible for the families and the ward personnel, dramatic changes in speed of discharge and other services to inpatients began to ensue. The group that I was working with then began to see other interdepartmental triangulation processes in which they were involved and took great delight in planning group moves which would have predictable and profound effects upon the organization. They were mental health workers, black and Hispanic, and loved sending the tensions and conflicts "back upstairs where they belonged." We got so good at it that we could predict, for example, that by refusing to engage in certain activities, the following week there would be a sharp clash between the so-called Cadre, a group of professionals who acted as advisors to the chief of service, and the day hospital. Finally, the conflicts travelled all the way back to the top and the chief resigned. The experience proved to my satisfaction that an organization is, indeed, a system in which change in any element reflects change in the whole.[3]

Still, the grasp of the whole organization as an organization eluded me. We had marvelously enhanced the well-being of the group with which I worked but the organization fell apart. It was the exact equivalent of treating a schizophrenic patient in the context of the family which greatly increased therapeutic effectiveness, but did not enhance the family as a family.

I believe that the jump from family to clan, from department to organization is much greater than the jump from individual to family because the organization is intrinsically inimical to the well-being of the individual. Most books on organizational development state that the goal of organizational development is to improve the organization and nurture the individual. For example, French and Bell state, "it is possible for the people within an organization collaboratively to manage the culture of that organization in such a way that the goals and purposes of the organization are attained at the same time that human values of individuals within the organization are furthered" (12). This statement I believe to be correct *as stated*, but it is often taken to mean that, as the same authors later say, "most organizations can profitably learn to be more responsive to organizational members" (13). In my view, much effort has been wasted on interventions calculated to make the organization more responsive to its individual members. The nature of an organization is that it doesn't nurture; only families or

[3]Unpublished study of effecting permanent changes in the organization of a total mental health care delivery system by working only with therapy aides.

small groups do that. The trick is to allow the organization to ignore the individual and empower its departments, teams, and other work groups to take care of their own. That is the subject of another book.

A second difficulty is that the processes and relationships of a clan or organization are much more complex than a family. Not only is there much more depth and span to an organization, that is, more lateral and vertical tiers of relationship, but most people operate in two or three groups at a time. We have to visualize a clan or organization as a series of pyramids. For example, while the chief or foreman of each team or department is involved in triangulation patterns within the team or department, he or she is also a peer in a group of middle managers and reports directly with others to a higher echelon manager. The strength of the middle managers' relationships with each other compared to their respective relationships with the general manager is extremely important to the well-being of the organization. Different organizations have characteristic differences in the balance of these relationships.

It is for the further discovery and elucidation of what will make our organizations work better that I think family therapists are admirably suited and they should and will pursue this study. We are already in the schools, the community and the extended family. It is time that we took some responsibility for the improved functioning of these entities as well as trying to use them in the furtherance of family therapy.

In fact, the continued well-being of families (indeed, humankind) demands that we enhance the systems in which they operate. Once a family gets "better," it needs to expand its purpose outward, for a family which is only about improving itself will have to continue having breakdowns in order to stay in business. This is the lesson that tells us that viability of the system is a function of its openness.

Just so, family therapy as a movement and family therapists as a body will need to move on very soon.

# References

1. Wittgenstein, Ludwig, *Tractatus Logico – Philosophicus.* Translated by D.F. Pears & B.F. McGuinness (London: Routledge & Kegan Paul, 1961), 151.

2. Einstein, Albert E., *Cosmic Religion* (New York: Covici Friede, 1931), 104.

3. Pater, Walter, *The Renaissance, Studies in Art and Poetry* (London: Macmillan and Co., 1910), 239.

4. Hoffman, Lynn, *Foundations of Family Therapy* (New York: Basic Books, Inc. 1981), 202.

5. Einstein, Albert, *Cosmic Religion*, 97.

6. Castaneda, Carlos, *Journey to Ixtlan*, (New York: Simon & Schuster, 1972), 10.

7. Erhard, Werner, *Creation: A Matter of Distinction*, (San Francisco: Audiotape, 1983).

8. Fuller, R. Buckminster, *Synergetics*, in collaboration with E.J. Applewhite, (New York: Macmillan Publishing Co. Inc. 1975), xxv-xxxi.

9. Berenson, Bernard, *Seeing and Knowing* (London: Chapman and Hall, 1953), 7.

10. Ibid, 7.

11. French, Wendell L. and Bell, Cecil H. Jr., *Organization Development* (New Jersey: Prentice-Hall Inc., 1973), xiii.

12. Ibid, 72.

# NAME INDEX

# SUBJECT INDEX